ROYAL LANCASTRIAN POTTERY, 1900-1938

Royal Lancastrian Pottery

1900-1938

Its achievements and its makers

By ABRAHAM LOMAX

(*Chemist at the Works* 1896-1911)

With 4 colour plates and 60 other illustrations

PUBLISHED BY

ABRAHAM LOMAX

AINSWORTH HOUSE, BREIGHTMET, BOLTON

1957

Printed in England by
TILLOTSONS (BOLTON) LIMITED
Bolton and London

*To all
who have revealed
some new facet
of truth and beauty
in the ancient and honourable
craft of the potter
this book is dedicated.*

Acknowledgements

I GRATEFULLY ACKNOWLEDGE my indebtedness to many for help willingly and generously given. Without their aid this book could not have been written. The willing co-operation of the Directors of Messrs. Pilkington's Tiles Limited and the facilities they afforded me helped considerably. To members of the Burton family; to several of my former colleagues at the pottery; to many correspondents; to the editors of the *Manchester Guardian* and the *Pottery Gazette* for permission to quote from their journals, and the *British Ceramic Society* and the *Royal Society of Arts* for a like privilege; to Mr. Reginald Haggar for permission to quote from his writings; to all who have loaned pottery and/or photographs or blocks for illustration; to the Director of the Manchester City Art Galleries for the privilege of using the Queen's Park Gallery for photographic purposes, and to Mr. A. B. Searle for helpful advice, my sincere thanks are hereby given.

I desire to make special mention of the valuable help given by Mr. Gordon M. Forsyth. He awakened in my mind the idea that someone should write a book recounting the achievements of the Pilkington factory. He manifested keen interest in the book's progress; offering criticism, suggestions, and encouragement. He refrained from mentioning anything about the part he played in making the ware famous. Only that portion of Chapter 4 which describes the atmosphere of the studio during his time is directly owed to him.

ABRAHAM LOMAX

Ainsworth House, Breightmet, Bolton

7

Contents

CONTENTS

SECTION FOUR: INDEBTEDNESS TO SCIENCE

List of Illustrations

11

Introduction

IN 1893 a brilliant scientist named William Burton was appointed technical and artistic head of a new tile works near Manchester. After establishing the business on a sound footing he turned his attention to the fulfilment of a long cherished ambition to make fine pottery on the lines of the ancient Chinese and Persian potters. He gathered round him a company of chemists, craftsmen and artists, and together they produced decorative pottery of most exceptional merit.

They had the good fortune to make some striking discoveries at a very early stage in their career; among them some new glazes possessing peculiar characteristics and also two entirely new coloured glazes with colours quite unlike anything hitherto produced by potters anywhere.

These developments came at a time when there were indications of a revolt against that part of late Victorian pottery which was heavily overladen with so-called decoration. A feeling after greater simplicity was abroad. Lancastrian Pottery met that need by demonstrating that beautiful line combined with fine glazing could dispense with added ornamentation and yet yield exquisitely beautiful pottery.

These early successes were soon followed by a really triumphant achievement. The elusive process of producing iridescent lustre painted pottery was mastered sufficiently to enable a relatively high proportion of successful pieces to be produced. Twenty years or so later another wonderful advance happened. A unique way of decorating pottery was discovered yielding pottery of exquisite charm. Truly, the Royal Lancastrian potters advanced the ART OF THE POTTER more than any other group ever did in so short a time.

13

INTRODUCTION

This book is an authentic account of the rise and development of
the ware written by one of the group of potters who started the
venture, and is totally unlike all other books on pottery. It is divided
into four sections, the first of which occupies four chapters and is in
narrative form. Beginning with the discovery of a bed of clay it con-
tinues with the inception of the idea of making tiles, the appointment of the master potter and the migration of a colony of artists
and craftsmen to start the venture. The next three chapters contain
a full description of the ware written in the order of its development
from the early experimental work that laid the foundation to the
cessation of manufacture in 1938. These three chapters correspond
to three striking advances in the art and technique of pottery
decoration achieved by the Lancastrian potters. The first was the
discovery of some entirely new glazes; the second the conquest of
the difficult art of producing iridescent lustre ware painted by
gifted artists, and the third the discovery of an entirely new way of
painting designs on pottery.

The second section contains fascinating stories of wonderful discoveries, some through chance or by accident, and others resulting
from diligent research. It also contains a very full account of the
difficulties experienced in the elusive art of producing iridescent
lustre decoration on pottery. It goes much further than detailing
the difficulties of the process. Drawing on the experiences of other
industries it offers what appears to be a sound explanation of the
formation of the iridescent film. No other book does this. All other
accounts, from Picolpasso's sixteenth-century manuscript down to
the latest book on the subject, tell what the potter does, but do not
explain how the iridescent film is formed. The section contains also
an absorbingly interesting and penetrating account of the unusual
factors resident in the new LAPIS ware.

The third section comprises a series of biographical sketches of
the people who produced the ware. Included are the two eminent
potters, William and Joseph Burton, who were the technical and

artistic heads; the chief designer, Gordon M. Forsyth; the thrower, E. T. Radford, and shorter notices of others. All these four men became pre-eminent in their respective careers. William Burton soon rose to be one of the leaders in the pottery industry and eventually became the most famous English potter since Josiah Wedgwood. Joseph Burton was endowed with a remarkable faculty of sensing the capabilities of pottery glazes. This, with his long and intimate experience of pottery making gradually developed a clear conception of the vital factors in the potter's craft which ultimately resulted in his writing what is doubtless the finest monograph ever written on *Quality in Pottery*. Gordon Forsyth is the artist who has exercised a greater influence on the Art side of English pottery than any other British artist, and Edward T. Radford was the most renowned thrower of his day. These men along with half a dozen talented assistants formed an incomparable group. Ceramic history contains nothing like it.

It is no wonder then that this group working in unison in the difficult art of fine decorative pottery making at a time when science was pouring out a wealth of new knowledge should produce pottery that was different from the styles in existence. The group did that when they produced Royal Lancastrian Pottery.

The concluding section acknowledges the debt that Royal Lancastrian Pottery owes to science. This is included because the period in which we are now living is a scientific age wherein the knowledge of science is widespread and readily understood and therefore knowledge of the important part contributed by science will be appreciated by many.

The book is unique among books on pottery because its contents are new. Royal Lancastrian Pottery surprised the world by its newness. It revealed fresh beauty residing in just fine line combined with colour. It brought forth new colours of surpassing beauty and new glazes with strange and exciting peculiarities. It astonished potters by these things and artists by its revival of the wonderful

15

iridescent lustre painted pottery of the ancients. It enlarged the field of artistic expression by the discovery of a unique way of painting designs in pottery. In Royal Lancastrian Pottery are combined science, art, craftsmanship and technique of the highest quality. Its makers were eminent in their respective spheres and by their efforts the art of the potter extended her borders.

Four coloured plates show four absolutely new coloured glazes; two of them being derivatives of the other two. In ceramics the advent of a new coloured glaze is an exceedingly rare event; hence, the discovery of two more is an unparalleled achievement. The other illustrations include several personal photographs and examples of the work of the principal artists.

> *A stranger here strange things doth meet,*
> *Strange glories see;*
> *Strange treasures lodged in this fair world appear,*
> *Strange all and new to me.*
>
> THOMAS TRAHERNE

SECTION

1

Origin

and

Development

CHAPTER 1

Early Days

Five MILES to the north of Manchester lies the township of Clifton, once a thriving colliery village. On its eastern side is the wide Irwell valley with its steep sloping sides. Along the western side of the valley is the railway line from Bolton to Manchester, and at the southern end of the township the railway from north-east Lancashire crosses the valley on a long line of arches and joins the line from Bolton. Hence, the locality is named Clifton Junction. Here, in 1892 the Lancastrian pottery works was built.

It came about this way. In 1889 the Clifton & Kersley Coal Co. began the sinking of a pair of pit shafts near to the site where the pottery was afterwards built. These sinkings were on the north side of the geological fault known as the Pendleton fault. It was intended to work the coal seams lying to the south of this fault, but owing to meeting excessive quantities of water the project was abandoned.

This Pendleton fault is a downthrow of strata of over 700 yards, and rocks known as the Permian Measures overlie the Coal Measures on the north of the fault. The sinking began in Permian strata and met with beds of marl (clay containing carbonate of lime).

The owners, four brothers named Pilkington, turned their attention to making use of the marl discovered in the sinking. Their first idea was to use it for making white and coloured glazed bricks since they were already successfully making common bricks with marl at one of their collieries nearby.

It happened that Mr. James Lee Wood, the secretary of the Coal Company, was acquainted with Mr. William Burton, then chemist

18

THE PENDLETON FAULT

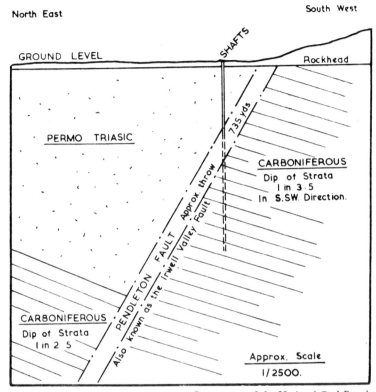

By courtesy of the National Coal Board.

at the famous firm of Messrs. Josiah Wedgwood & Sons. He suggested that Mr. Burton be asked to test the marl and report on its capabilities. Samples of the marl were sent to him. Based on the results of his tests many larger scale experiments for glazed bricks were made at the colliery brickworks. Later, Mr. Burton suggested that the manufacture of tiles would be preferable because there was an expanding market, and makers were finding it very profitable. He believed they could go one better than some of the existing tile manufacturers, for architects were asking for better things than were then being made.

In 1891 a definite proposal was made that he should leave Messrs. Wedgwoods, but as the conditions of his engagement with them did not allow him to leave before the term expired in 1892, his migration did not take place until then.

The site chosen for the factory had many advantages. It was a large area of level land bordered on two sides by a canal, which made it an ideal position for an industry using water-borne raw materials such as South of England clays and stone, and imported flints and feldspar. Transport by rail also was close at hand. It would be a simple matter to connect the works to the main line. Finally, there was abundant coal within easy reach.

As further experiments showed that the marl then being used for brickmaking was also suitable for the manufacture of flooring tiles and, therefore, there was no particular need for the marl found in the sinkings, these were abandoned and the shafts filled up. Thus, one venture failed but started another which prospered abundantly.

The factory was planned for the dual purpose of manufacturing tiles for walls, floors, fireplaces, etc. by the clay dust compression process, and for making architectural faience from moist clay. It was well laid out for the purpose and provision was made for extensions should they become necessary.

To this carefully planned, spacious, and well equipped modern factory came a colony of key-workers, all of them expert in their particular spheres. There was a miller, a slip maker, some tile makers, a saggar maker, some biscuit, glost, and majolica placers, firemen, warehousemen and packers, a moulder, faience makers, an engraver, a modeller, a printer, some dippers and painters and paintresses. There was, too, a departmental manager and a chief designer.

The coming of the industry enriched the district in many ways. Hitherto, the chief industries of the locality were coal mining and cotton spinning. Neither of these could be said to be attractive occupations in those days. This new industry opened a door to a wider world—a world of beauty. Pottery, particularly pottery concerned with form and colour and artist's adornment, awakened a new interest, brought gifted and brilliant men and women of high artistic ability and scientific attainments, and provided opportunities for many to live a creative life.

The leader of the new venture, William Burton, was talented to an exceptional degree. Rarely have men so young as he, and with so short a working experience, been invited to accept such great responsibility as he undertook in going to Clifton Junction. The locality lacked the traditions of the new industry. Where an industry is localised, as pottery is in North Staffordshire and cotton is in parts of Lancashire, the atmosphere is charged with tradition. Conversation in the home, the club, the school, the street—every place where folk gather is steeped in the lingo. Consequently, there is an aptitude—a readiness—which fits the people for the industry. Some other winsome force was needed if labour was to be attracted. It came in William Burton's personality. The essentials of success were in his make-up. 'He came; he saw; he conquered.' With him came his brother, Joseph, and the two were colleagues until William retired in 1915.

The new occupations had to establish themselves in popularity with the local working classes if a continual supply of workers was to be forthcoming. The venture was looked at askance by many parents at first, but as the works progressed and more and more workers found that there was always full employment at favourable wages, hesitation gave place to welcome. Ere long, two, three, four, and even more members of families found employment there.

On the 13th of January 1893, William Hiley, in the presence of Mr. Edward and Mr. Charles Pilkington, set the engine in motion for the first time. From then on, apart from the serious interruptions of two World Wars, the record is one of almost continuous growth and development. Its employees now number over 800.

21

CHAPTER 2

CHAPTER 2

First Period, 1900-1904

The story of Royal Lancastrian Pottery really begins with William Burton, who, at the age of 24 left the Royal School of Mines and joined the staff of the famous pottery of Josiah Wedgwood & Sons at Etruria, in the Potteries district of North Staffordshire. He soon felt the fascination and charm of this age-old craft and quickly began to extend his knowledge of it. Being keenly interested he spent some of his holidays visiting other potteries, and even working on some. This enabled him to make the acquaintance of other potters and learn from their experiences. He also visited many museums to study the works of ancient potters. He read both extensively and intensively. His five years at Wedgwoods, from 1887 to 1892, added technical and practical training. He was thus well equipped for later confidently adventuring his future in the industry. His talents, education, training and experience waited upon opportunity. Waiting was brief. His coming to Clifton Junction at the invitation of Messrs. Pilkington was timely and fortunate. The splendid collaboration between them heralded success. With their continual interest, encouragement and support he bounded forward.

Early in his career as a potter he became acquainted with the eminent potter, Bernard Moore, and was very much impressed by his successful reproduction of some of the more famous glazes of Oriental potters, particularly flambé and turquoise. It may have been this association with Bernard Moore that inspired William Burton to attempt similar reproductions. If this association did not initiate the idea in his mind it certainly intensified his longing to make the attempt.

William Burton's early years at Clifton Junction were occupied with the many problems involved in the founding of a new industry, and so it was not until 1897 that a start could be made with pottery as distinct from tiles. He began in a small way making a variety of articles such as tops for hat pins, buttons, moulded vases, etc., for which purpose he engaged a potter named Tunnicliffe, who previously had made pots for the famous artist potter, Marc L. Solon, at Mintons.

Soon afterwards he introduced decoration by painting on pots bought in the biscuit state (already fired but not glazed). These were made by John Thomas Firth at Kirkby Lonsdale, a town in Westmorland many centuries old. When a young man, Firth became interested in art, did some painting, attended art classes and grew fond of modelling. He made himself a throwing wheel worked by a foot pedal. His small workshop on the bank of the river Lune, at the bottom of Mill Brow, is now in ruins. He got red clay from Burton, a village a few miles away, where pottery was then made. Later he mixed this red clay with white, obtaining china clay for the purpose from Messrs. Wengers of Stoke-on-Trent, from whom he also got his pigments and glazes. Afterwards he used mainly a creamy white body. By chance he discovered how to make an unglazed vitreous black ware, specimens of it being exhibited in London. He blunged (agitated with water) and sieved his clays by hand. In the early days he sent his pots to Burton to be fired but later built himself a kiln in the basement underneath his workroom. At times his son Sydney assisted him, and his daughter Ellen decorated much of the ware in *Sgraffito** style. All three scratched their initials on the base of their particular pots, JTF   SF   EF.
                                        KL   KL   KL

* Producing a two-colour design by cutting or incising through a coating of clay of one colour and thereby exposing the colour of the body underneath.

Evidently they were potters of some repute for illustrations of their work appeared in *The Studio, The Journal of the Society of Arts,* and in the *Journal of Decorative Art*. Examples were purchased by the Victoria and Albert Museum.

The Firth family were great admirers of William Burton and interchange of visits took place. Joseph Burton was also a friend of the family. The first three of the Firth pots decorated at the Lancastrian Pottery works were painted by Miss Briggs.

Some of the Lancastrian pieces made in these formative days were exhibited at the Paris exhibition of 1900. They included blocks of architectural faience, tiles of various sorts, a few pots, and a pair of 'Sunstone'* glazed lions made from the original mould of Alfred Stevens for the lions that sat on the iron railings surrounding the British Museum. William Burton took a party of his young artists to the exhibition that they might see the works of contemporary Continental potters.

All these were indications of ripening fruition of William Burton's long cherished hopes and aspirations. Artists and artisans were becoming accustomed to pots as well as tiles. Experience and skills were accumulating. Pitfalls inherent in the new processes were being located. There was an atmosphere of expectancy about, not only at Pilkington's, but at other English potteries and also on the Continent. Especially was this so in the realm of coloured glazes— no doubt partly due to their rapidly growing use on tiles for architectural purposes.

All down the centuries since primitive man began to make pottery, and especially after he began to coat it with glaze, men have been delighted with its wondrous beauties. The potters of long ago looked about them to see what Nature had that they could use. They stumbled on riches which, in the hands of adventurous men yielded new textures, qualities, colours and ways of decoration. The world owes much to these unnamed pioneers, whose works do follow

---

* Glaze crowded with a myriad of glistening crystals.

1. The piece of saggar coated with melted frit.
Length 2¾ in. Width 1½ in.

Author's collection

2. Striated, veined and feathered light bluish green opalescent glaze on light red body.

Height 16¼ in.

Victoria and Albert Museum, Crown copyright

5. Veined and feathered light bluish green opalescent glaze on light red body.
Height 9½ in.

4. White flocks in transparent deep cobalt blue glaze.
Height 7 in.

them. 'Other men laboured, and we are entered into their labours.'

By the end of the nineteenth century the world had, in its known pottery glazes, a wealth of colour that art and skill were daily using for the enrichment of life. Little did potters, even adventurous potters, think then that in the offing, awaiting the favourable breeze, were argosies laden with other new and precious things. Yet, as the bursting of a flower bud releases a blaze of colour, so the sudden appearance of new beauties in pottery glazes at the beginning of this twentieth century unveiled latent possibilities, and heralded the dawn of a new era of pottery adornment. The credit for this notable advance belongs chiefly to Pilkington's Lancastrian Pottery.

A stroke of good fortune brought Lancastrian Pottery to birth. In July 1903 an accident happened which yielded a surprising and exciting glaze effect. At this period several trials of glaze frits (glassy material) having differing compositions were being made. The procedure was to mix intimately their components; place the

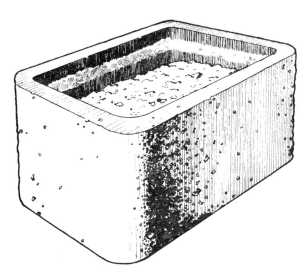

Flint-lined saggar containing mixture of materials to make a glaze frit.

25

mixture inside a flint-lined saggar* and fire it in a glost oven. Many such trials were made but none of them gave exactly what was wanted. So a mixture differing considerably from the others was tried. During the firing of this frit mixture of unusual composition a small quantity bubbled over and a small area of the outside of the saggar became coated with a thin layer of the molten glass. On cooling, this became a beautiful delicately veined opalescent glaze, though the mass of the frit was perfectly transparent. Here was something new!

The frit proved to be very interesting; it was unusually hard to break and when struck rang like a bell. An addition of 8% of copper oxide to the mixture before fritting was made in the expectation that a bluish-green frit would result, but no; the resultant frit was practically colourless. The copper had separated out in the form of more or less spherical globules of metallic copper located chiefly in the lower part—an amazing result. The normal uncoloured frit when ground and applied as a glaze produced wonderfully beautiful glazes, especially when coloured by the addition of the usual colouring oxides. In Chapter 5 is a fuller description of these marvellous glazes and a suggested explanation of the peculiar properties of the glaze.

During several weeks following this exciting event many trials were made of additions of various materials to the ground frit. Some most extraordinary glaze effects resulted. Their unusual character can be judged from a few sentences taken from my experiment note book of that period. In it were recorded particulars of the trials as they were made and the results when they came forth. Here are some: 'Magnificent results.' 'Full of sparkling crystals.' 'Indescribable for effect of broken variegated opalescent colours; iron ones especially.'

Plate No. 1 shows the actual piece of sagger with its coating of

---

* A fireclay container to hold pottery to protect it during the firing operation. The name is derived from 'Safe-guard'.

glaze. When it was shown to William and Joseph Burton both obviously became excited for both of them saw beauty and promise in it. These beautiful and exciting new glaze effects made such a powerful impression on William Burton that he felt that the opportune moment for launching out on the manufacture of decorative pottery had arrived. The decision to start making decorative glazed pottery was made in October 1903. The first trial batch of clay for throwing proved satisfactory. A bulk quantity was made in November. In that month a throwing wheel was installed and E. T. Radford, the thrower, arrived. *In November* 1903 *the large scale manufacture of Lancastrian Pottery began.*

William Burton summarily described what brought about the sudden change from dabbling at pottery to definite purposeful activity when, replying to a vote of thanks after delivering a lecture before the Royal Society of Arts in London on 10th May 1904, he said he was primarily a tile maker, and he had only turned to pottery making because he had to; so many effects were produced that were beautiful in themselves, but absolutely useless on the surface of a tile; it was necessary to have a rounded surface to show them off.

The accidental overflowing of a frit in fusion brought Lancastrian Pottery to birth. Had the frit not overflowed, the manufacture of pottery on an industrial scale would have been started sooner or later, for so much preparatory work had been done, but we might have missed all the extraordinary glaze effects that followed it, and the arrival of Lancastrian Pottery would not have been so startling as it was.

The name given to the new ware—LANCASTRIAN—is highly appropriate. The factory is located in the County of Lancaster; its proprietors scions of an historic Lancashire family; and both its directing heads (William and Joseph Burton) were Lancashire born and bred.

The venture had an auspicious start. In six months time progress was so great that an exhibition could be staged in London. This rapid progress was assisted by using some new glazes which had been discovered a few years earlier and which were being successfully used on flat tiles. They proved to be highly successful when applied to the rounded shapes of this new pottery ware. Thus it came about that 'Sunstone' and 'Eggshell' glazed pottery were among the early products of Lancastrian Pottery. In June 1904, the first examples of the ware were publicly exhibited. The exhibition caused quite a sensation among potters, connoisseurs, lovers of Art and of beautiful pottery, and also the general public. The shapes were true pottery-shapes, characterised by simplicity and directness, without twisted handles or other abnormalities. The thrown pots appeared to be the natural outcome of spinning clay on a revolving table with the workman's hands in control. The glazes, with perhaps one exception, were not harsh or stark but mellow. Those of a glassy character had their brilliance toned down by opalescence or other effects. It was an exhibition solely of pottery shapes and glazes entirely devoid of added ornamentation by painters, modellers, or other artists—just simple line and fine glazing—yet it created an extraordinary impression.

According to press reports the exhibition 'was a bewildering carnival of perfect colours applied on comely and appropriate shapes, based on Greek, Persian, or Chinese forms. A few, one a queer poisonous blue (Plate A) seemed to sing out above the others, but artistic sense was aroused and quickened, not disturbed. In a great room draped with white were vases, bowls, dishes and trays, resplendent in all the colours of the rainbow and glittering like precious stones. Wherever one turned one was delighted with an indescribable variety of exquisite hues, ranging from faint pink and sky blue to the richest purple and dark green and amber. There was, too, a whole series of opalescent and crystalline effects which surpass anything attempted before. None need desire anything finer than these wonderful opalescent glazes, whose strife in the great heat draws themselves into fine lines and visible relief; or the tall octagonal jars with their perfect lines and fine feathering, or the sunstone glaze with the deep glint of innumerable crystals. What these can do in the way of actual application may be seen by the great lions cast from an original mould of Alfred Stevens and now upstanding with a fine dignity and new but exquisite colour'.

There was much more of similar exuberant language, which goes to show how great was the surprise, the wonder, and amazement aroused by the immense variety of colour, texture, and novel effects in these new pottery glazes.

The texture glazes, so called from the special quality of 'feel' and appearance of the glaze, had a surface and gloss like the surface of an eggshell or vellum. This type of glaze had received a good deal of attention at the factory during the preceding ten years. Those described as fruit-skin glazes had a surface resembling that of a pear, or melon, or apricot, or orange, with colour varying from pale lemon to deep russet, or from apple green to olive brown, as on the natural fruit.

Texture glazes were not confined to surface effects. There was internal as well as external texture. These were named *Transmutation glazes*. Some of these effects were produced during firing by the glazes themselves without any artificial stimulation; others were manipulated by expert glazers.

Beautiful curdled effects were obtained by applying two layers of glaze, the underneath one being heavily loaded with oxide of tin, and the top one a transparent coloured glaze, the effect being enhanced by using shapes that allowed the glaze to gather in hollows or channels. This two-layer method offers an enormous variety of effects to the explorer. When it is remembered that Pilkingtons eventually had a multitude of glazes of widely differing composition and character, it is no wonder that their range of curdled, mottled, flocculent, and clouded texture glazes, was, like Joseph's coat of many colours, the admiration of many and the envy of others.

29

This new style of decorative pottery, with its emphasis on colour, was in keeping with and helped forward the change in taste that applied art was experiencing. Potters, dyers, textile designers and others, in this and other countries were awakening to the value of colour and colour 'effects'. Ideas were simmering in the minds of progressive potters, and several succeeded in reviving the old or in bringing forward something new. 'Tiger Eye' crystalline glazes were produced at Rookwood, U.S.A. Theodore Deck in France produced pottery in the style of the Ancient Persians, so did William de Morgan here. At the Paris exhibition of 1900, glazes bearing radiating crystals on their surface were shown. Bernard Moore in Staffordshire was producing fine *Rouge Flambé* glazes and coloured glazed ware was being made by Howson Taylor at Birmingham. After the turn of the century, Messrs. Doulton put their well-known Flambé glazed pottery on the market in 1910, and in 1913, Mr. Moorcroft began producing his fine 'Powder Blue' glazed ware. In the midst of this ferment Lancastrian Pottery made its startling appearance. It seemed to gather up in one whole the gropings of many and added to them its own new and beautiful creations. Coloured glazed ware became an important section of the pottery industry. Just as Josiah Wedgwood was the outstanding potter in a group developing English Earthenware and therefore his name is linked with it, so Lancastrian is the outstanding name in the group of those who contributed to this striking development of coloured glazed ware.

CHAPTER 3

Second Period, 1904-1908

THE SUCCESS so soon achieved intensified interest and zeal. Researches continued and were rewarded with other successes. Within the space of another three years two other new coloured glazes—Uranium Orange and Uranium Orange Vermilion—were discovered, flambé glazes were produced, and, finest of all, the elusive art of producing iridescent lustre was rediscovered. William Burton with the collaboration of his brother Joseph and the aid of a skilful and responsive fireman thus realised his long-cherished ambition of producing pottery painted by gifted artists and issuing from the kiln with enchanting iridescence. His trials commenced in January 1903. They were devised by him and carried out by the laboratory chemist, Norman Sinclair. The firing was done in an ordinary laboratory gas fired muffle, rice carbon being used to produce the reducing atmosphere. In 1906 a specially designed muffle-kiln* was built and production in quantity began.

To succeed in producing iridescent lustre painting on pottery is a great achievement, for it demands great skill to stain into an already fired glaze some compound of silver or copper so as to produce a film of metal perfectly incorporated with the glaze, yet of such exquisite tenuity that it glows with all the iris-colours of a soap bubble, a piece of mother-of-pearl or a peacock's feather—colours which change in a fascinating way with every change of viewpoint giving a:

* A closed firing chamber not penetrated by flames. These pass underneath and up the outsides of the firebrick casing.

Surface shimmering with rainbow hues,
Purple and crimson and turquoise blues,
Ruby and orange, yellow and green;
Each of them deck'd in glorious sheen.

It was immediately realised that here was scope for artists of the highest class. There were several artists on the staff at the time, designing and painting tiles and wall plaques, but none were of the calibre needed to guide artistic development in the new medium. So William Burton sought for someone capable of such a high mission; it was a momentous choice he had to make.

The position being offered was attractive and desirable for several reasons. It was an invitation to be the pioneer artist in the development of a new style of pottery decoration—a fine opportunity for a man of ideas and such opportunities are rare indeed! He would be in association with one of the most distinguished potters of the time. He would be at a factory with a rapidly rising reputation. He would find ready at hand craftsmen of several kinds, including expert potters, modellers, mould-makers and glazers using glazes and colours that had proved their quality through years of testing experience. He would find hundreds of pottery shapes being made. He would have at his command a group of artist painters well-versed in the conditions current in the factory. Moreover, the height already reached by Lancastrian ware was a solid foundation for loftier flights. Iridescent lustre was calling loudly for some talented artist to display her charms. He had but to step in, look around, then begin to play his role: fortunate man! William Burton consulted Bernard Moore, who introduced him to Gordon M. Forsyth (then with Minton Hollins & Co., Tile Manufacturers) whom he forthwith engaged to take charge of the existing staff of artists. It was both a great responsibility and a severe test for one only 25 years of age.

To get a correct picture of the art side of the firm's activities it is necessary to return to the beginning of 1893 when the first two

5. Plaster cast of **St. George and the Dragon.** Designed by G. M. Forsyth.
Modelled by R. Joyce.
Height 16 in. Width 42 in.

Author's collection

Leading group

TISIPHONE

9. Tisiphone: one of the three Euminides who mercilessly drove guilty
souls to the gates of the dismal dark abyss of Tartarus. Painted by G. M.
Forsyth.   *By courtesy of the Lord Dunsany*

artists arrived. They were John Chambers and A. J. (Joseph) Kwiatkowski. Both were among the earliest members of the staff to arrive at Clifton Junction.

Joseph Kwiatkowski was recommended to William Burton by a Mr. Allen, of Wedgwoods, who knew him as a modeller and painter working on his own and, at the same time, studying for an art scholarship to South Kensington. He modelled tiles and plaques and panels, both from his own designs and from those of other designers. He was mainly occupied with this class of work, and consequently, he contributed very little to Lancastrian ware and that only in its early years.

John Chambers was the first designer and also head of the architectural faience department. The rapid growth of the firm and its widening activities brought about a separation of these two functions. A new department to handle the large scale tiling jobs was formed under Mr. F. C. Howells with a staff of draughtsmen; he retired in 1915, and was succeeded by John Hurdley who retained the position until he retired in 1946. This change did not relieve John Chambers completely of architectural matters; in fact, he dealt with top ranking architects on special matters until his retirement at Christmas, 1938. The work involved in tile designing, in conferences with consultant designers like Lewis F. Day, Walter Crane, and C. F. A. Voysey, in supervising the modeller, the engraver, the mould-makers, and his staff provided scope for his talents and occupied much of his time. However, he was able to give some time in the early days to Lancastrian ware, particularly in designing shapes. Joseph Burton had a high opinion of his work in this, and often said so. The most notable of the shapes introduced by Mr. Chambers was the very popular kylix based on an ancient Greek shape.

The artists employed by the firm in the period 1900-1938 are listed below. All the women artists had had some art training before joining the firm. The dates given refer to men only. Of those named

33

in the list, the Misses Tyldsley, Briggs, Yates, Storey and Hughes had left before Gordon Forsyth arrived. Charles Cundall, George Ormrod, and Miss Burton came later. Besides these there were many young women employed in painting tiles with majolica glazes.

ARTISTS OF THE PERIOD 1900-1938

1893	John Chambers	Miss Ruth Tyldsley
1893	A. J. (Joseph) Kwiatkowski	Miss Kate Briggs
1894	William S. Mycock	Miss Dorothy Dacre
1895?	Thomas F. Evans	Miss Annie Yates
?	Edward Kent	Miss Annie Storey
?	Albert Barlow	Miss Fanny Hughes
?	Albert Hall	Miss Jessie Jones
1905	Richard Joyce	Miss Gwladys M. Rodgers
1906	Gordon M. Forsyth	Miss Annie Burton
1907	Charles E. Cundall	
1917	George Ormrod	

Gordon Forsyth found the personal climate invigorating, for his new colleagues were all 'good companions'. They were cheery, sociable, enthusiastic and, as he said afterwards, all of them were fine artists. They were, however, as sheep without a shepherd, needing someone to direct their efforts to a common purpose, and bind their incoherent activities into a unity.

His influence was soon manifest. Lustre ware took on a 'new look'. It was painted chiefly by G. M. Forsyth, Will Mycock, Charles Cundall, Richard Joyce, and Gwladys Rodgers. They raised the ware to, and maintained it at, a high level of excellence and it is to them that its fame is largely due. They enshrined in it their ideals, their outlook, their spirit; they gave it a stamp, a character, a unity, that distinguished it from all other decorative pottery; something that causes beholders to exclaim, 'That's Lancastrian'. Some of the other artists contributed, and the eminent designer Walter Crane designed some characteristic pieces.

Pilkingtons were more fortunately placed for exploiting the artistic possibilities of this process than were earlier potters, for they had available many more types of glazes, both coloured and colourless, and also glazes of more varied textures. With this much wider range of coloured grounds at their service the artists were able to produce effects such as the ancient potters never conceived. By applying a new and distinctive style of design on these backgrounds the artists at times produced pieces equalling those of the Persian, Spanish and Italian potters.

So far this chapter has been mainly concerned with the development of the wondrous iridescent lustre ware, but the fact should not be overlooked that development work with the coloured and other glazes was continued during this period and proved highly successful. The period 1904-1908 was certainly 'crowned with goodness'; in it the ware advanced in stature and in favour with collectors and connoisseurs and its fame spread far and wide. The opalescent and crystalline glazes, the fruit-skin and other texture-glazes, and the variegated transmutation-glazes increased in number and variety. In fact, progress continued all along the line.

It was a period of feverish activity. Everyone concerned was keenly interested and enthusiastic. The laboratory, the lead-house, the artists' studio, the craftsmen's shops, and the Board Room were hives of activity. People were bursting with ideas and energy, and everyone was rejoicing at the signal success. It was good to be alive in those days!

Progress was so rapid that by 1908 another public exhibition could be held. The Franco-British exhibition of that year provided the opportunity. The display of Lancastrian Pottery there was on a grand scale, being housed in a specially designed pavilion with walls covered with Persian-style tiles and floors of vitreous, unglazed white porcelain. The Lancastrian products, like those in the previous exhibition, made a sensational impression. There were many fine examples of the new glazes and a magnificent display of lustre decorated pots including five large vases painted by Gordon Forsyth worthy of special mention because they are among the firm's masterpieces. According to *The Exhibition Review* the finest is a tall vase of rich cobalt blue, flawless in surface, and painted with a bold design in silver lustre of the Ride of the Valkyries. The adaptation of the design to the form of the vase, the masterly drawing, and the peculiar transparency of the lustre, which experience can never absolutely guarantee to come out right, make this piece a remarkable specimen more worthy of a national museum than a private collection (Plates 6, 7, 8). Scarcely less fine is another large blue vase painted with a scene of Orpheus and the beasts. Next to which is a very dark green one decorated with an early ship and a motto across the back. ('They that go down to the sea in ships, that do business in great waters; These see the works of the Lord, and his wonders in the deep.') The effect of the lustre against this sombre ground is very fine, and is repeated in another large specimen divided into panels by vertical ribs of lustre and decorated with floral scrolls.

The largest vase in the collection is one of a splendid scarlet red, rather a trying colour perhaps in a decorative scheme, which is magnificently painted with an Æschylean scene of the three Euminides (Furies), in golden lustre perfectly adapted to the rounded curves of the ground. This competes for mastery with a no less imposing specimen 24-in. high, of pale blue body decorated with a raised and modelled representation of St. George and the Dragon. By a happy accident of the firing the golden lustre on the armour of the saint, and incidentally, his face as well, glow like burnished brass, whilst the Dragon's wings reflect a myriad iridescent rays (Plate 5). Another similar vase had the figures in red on a grey-blue mottled ground.

The exhibition also had some fine examples of the work of Richard Joyce, an artist-potter of exceptional ability. Two of them were designed by Walter Crane in his characteristic style. One is the 'Bon Accorde' vase shown on Plate 15. The other is a large vase with medium green ground with four draped female figures holding festoons and in between them in silver lustre are pedestal trays on which are dark red fires burning.

From these two last chapters readers will have gathered a fair idea of the wares produced in the early years of the venture. In the brief space of time from November 1903 when they began in earnest the manufacture of decorative pottery to 1908 when they astonished the world by the amazing display of ceramic master-pieces, the Lancastrian potters achieved unparalleled success and made an indelible impression on ceramic history. Right on to the outbreak of World War I superb examples of the potter's art con-tinued to come forth from the kilns.

It is noteworthy that during the first period the pottery was the work of artisans, craftsmen and chemists. No call was made upon painters or modellers. In the second period it was similar work enriched with artist's genius and skill.

The St. George and Dragon was designed by Gordon Forsyth and modelled by Richard Joyce in the form of a slab 44 inches by 16 inches. A plaster mould was made from this model so that copies of the design in relief could be made in clay for transference to plain vases. Only two vases were thus ornamented. It was felt that more use should be made of this masterpiece of art and craftsmanship than just the decoration of two vases, so six plaster casts of the slab were made and presented to the following members of the staff: David Burton, Joseph Burton, Gordon M. Forsyth, John Chambers, William S. Mycock, and myself.

37

CHAPTER 4

Third Period, 1908-1938

THE FIRST TWENTY YEARS of this period were dominated by artists.
There was little call upon the chemist for anything new. So poten-
tially rich were the existing glazes that there was little need to
explore further. Actually, no chemist was employed in connection
with the control of processes and the prosecution of research from
January 1912 to November 1927. There was, however, a laboratory
chemist doing analytical and similar work. Reliable workmen like
Charles Dodd, John Bramwell, and William Rushton were given
the firm's standard recipes. They blended the clays, compounded
the colours, and prepared the glazes. Lancastrian pottery was then
a healthy child and appeared, for a time, to be able to dispense with
the support of a chemist.

Gordon M. Forsyth's arrival on the scene was the arrival of a
personality, possessed of ideals, ideas, and power. His advent
marked a revolutionary change in the history of decorative pottery
in England.

Firstly: the thrower was encouraged to produce individual pieces.
Hitherto the shapes had been designed or selected by others and
the thrower copied them. Now he was free to add his own con-
ceptions. Obviously he needed guidance in his newly acquired
freedom and both William Burton and Gordon Forsyth gladly
helped him along.

Secondly: the artists were encouraged to produce individual
designs and to mark the pieces with their monogram and with
something to indicate the year when they were painted. This

development was important and was later followed by other pottery firms. The pottery of the nineteenth century has many signed pieces, but the practice was not general—rather the reverse, for anonymity was a characteristic of that period.

The innovation which, in essence, was a revolt against mass production, was greatly appreciated, particularly by American retailers. They demanded what they called 'christened' productions with the designer's name as well as that of the firm incorporated in the piece.

The artist's personal marks and the firm's marks are reproduced on the next page. The artist's date marks included such signs as anchors, birds, rabbits, stags, swans, crossed swords. The key to these is lost. The two that I know to be certain are the R.A.F. wings used by G. M. Forsyth in the period 1919-1920, and the flaming torch used by him in 1913-14. On some pieces are two personal marks. This happens when the design is by one person and the painting by another. Pieces with designs by Walter Crane have his well-known mark as well as the mark of the painter.

Pieces made previous to or early in 1904 have either no mark at all or the letter 'P' incised. From 1904 until the cessation of manufacture the markings were generally standard, some of the following being used.

1. A NUMBER IN ORDINARY NUMERALS. These numbers began in 1905 at 2001 and continued until making ceased in 1937, with the exception that among the pieces marked E.T.R. (see No. 10 following) there are some with smaller numbers. In the author's collection are three numbered respectively 179, 203A, 226. They indicate the shape and size, and were useful to purchasers ordering repeats.

2. THE FIRM'S MARK. The first one, used in the period 1904-1913, is a combination of the two letters 'PL' with two bees. The letters are obviously for Pilkington and Lancastrian. The two bees, as the sound of the word indicates, represent the Burtons.

1904-1915

G. M. FORSYTH

GWLADYS RODGERS

TUDOR ROSE
1914-1938

W. S. MYCOCK

DOROTHY DACRE

LEWIS F. DAY
Designer

R. JOYCE

JESSIE JONES

WALTER CRANE
Designer

C. E. CUNDALL

ANNIE BURTON

MARKS AND MONOGRAMS

40

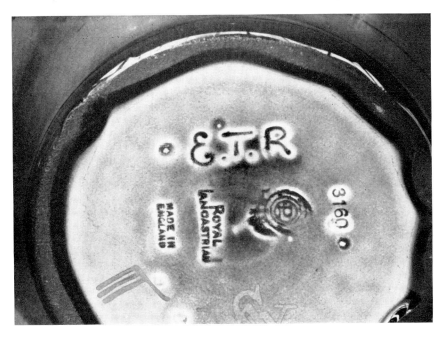

[See page 41]

11. Painted by
G. M. Forsyth.
*By courtesy of
Messrs. Pilkington's
Tiles Ltd.*

12. A true 14th century
shape. Painted by
G. M. Forsyth.
Height 5½ in.
*By courtesy of
Miss L. Lomax*

13. Both painted by R. Joyce.
Height (left) 6½ in. plus lid.
Author's collection

Height (right) 6½ in.
By courtesy of Mrs. G. Auckland

14. Painted by R. Joyce.
Height 9½ in.

By courtesy of Mrs. L. A. Pettiner

15. Designed by Walter Crane. Painted by R. Joyce.
Height 9 in.

By courtesy of Mrs F. C. Ormerod

16. Designed by Walter Crane. Painted by R. Joyce.
Height 10½ in.   *By courtesy of Mrs. L. A. Pettiner*

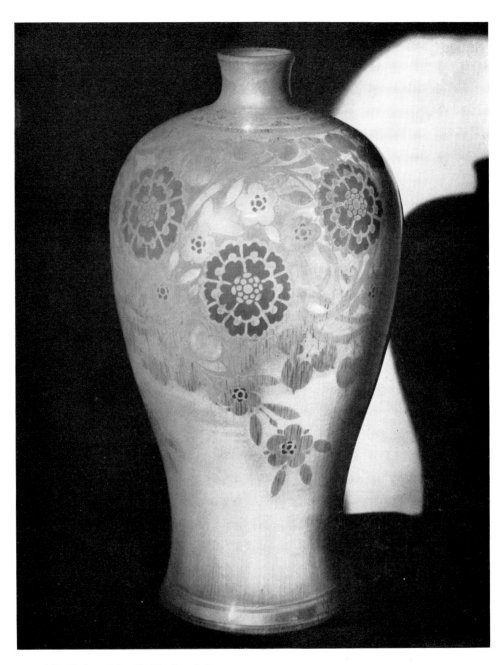

17. Painted by C. E. Cundall.
Height 11 in.   *By courtesy of Manchester Art Galleries Committee*

Height 5½ in.

Height 7 in.

Height 5½ in.

Author's collection

18. Painted by C. E. Cundall

19. Liverpool Museum damaged by bombing.

By courtesy of The Museums Association

It was designed by Lewis F. Day and was applied by transfer printing for about twelve months. Afterwards, it was impressed. In 1913, it was superseded by the Tudor Rose, which is the emblem of the Dukes of Lancaster.

3. A NUMBER IN ROMAN NUMERALS. This was used 1905-1913. It indicates the year in this century when the piece was made in the clay state.

4. THE PAINTER'S MONOGRAM.

5. THE PAINTER'S DATE EMBLEM.

6. THE DESIGNER'S MONOGRAM, if other than the painter.

7. ROYAL LANCASTRIAN.

8. MADE IN ENGLAND.

9. ENGLAND.

10. Initials E.T.R. were incised by Edward T. Radford on pieces thrown by him shortly before he retired.

A small 'x' appears on many pieces made in the period 1900-1918. This indicates that a potter named Bray had some part in making the clay shape. It may have been just the sponging of a thrown pot which had been turned and polished in the turning, or some slight carving of the piece, or making slight depressions. Far more numerous than these are the pieces he made complete, as a presser. Similarly, but in far fewer instances, a small 'v' is seen. This is the mark of R. Tunnicliffe, who did similar work.

Finally; some people have thought that the colour of the smear of glaze on the base of a piece had some significance. It had none whatever. The worker used any glaze that happened to be nearby at the time.

The suggestion to the thrower to be less dependent on forms provided for him and to put more of himself into the pot was not something out of the ordinary so far as Forsyth was concerned; it was the outflowing of his innate disposition. He seems to have been possessed with an irresistible urge to impart his spirit to his associates. By word of mouth and by example, he encouraged his staff to let their personality display itself in their productions.

His painters were a group of magnificent craftsmen, and the firm had the good sense to leave them free to develop their own ideas, which possibly is one reason why Royal Lancastrian ware made such a notable contribution to pottery. The spirit behind their production was the same as that which inspired the splendid work of all the historic styles.

Though each one was at liberty to develop his own ideas, all availed themselves of ideas floating through the studio. The group was a community with a common purpose, and it worked in harmonious co-operation. A *motif* introduced by one was not regarded by him or by the others as his exclusive property. For instance, Forsyth sometimes used an old print of Columbus's ship, the *Santa Maria*, and Mycock used the same *motif* on many of his pieces.

The liberty accorded to the artists shocked some people, especially those who held the view that designing and painting were two distinct branches of art, and that, in the main, a man was either the one or the other, and should keep within his particular province. For instance, Lewis F. Day, well-known for his books on pattern-designing, apparently had as his motto: 'Let me design and let who will execute.' He was horrified at the idea of all the artists painting their own original designs straight on to glazes suitably made for lustre treatment. He honestly thought it could not be done and said, 'It's all very well, but Forsyth cannot go on producing an individual design for every piece for much more than twelve months'. The reply to that is that not only Forsyth but all the staff managed to do this for the whole period of their service.

The firm did not overlook the necessity to nourish the mind and spirit of the Art staff. Good books on art and pottery were at their disposal. One of the many fine books provided was the classic work of Sarre and Martin, '*Mohammedanischer Kunst*'—an expensive work in three volumes containing a great collection of well-chosen examples of Mohammedan art magnificently reproduced in colour.

42

The studio became a hive of industry where artists from far and near foregathered. Lovers of art, whether practising or not, were constantly arriving to see the beautiful creations. Occasionally they would suggest ideas and sometimes try their skill on a pot.

The interest that Lancastrian pottery had aroused was widespread. Many people, particularly cultured people, availed themselves of the willingness of the firm to admit visitors and show them the processes of manufacture. The works was a magnet drawing artists, scientists, persons distinguished in academic and civic life, as well as potters and connoisseurs. Many stayed overnight at 'The Hollies' (the home of Mr. and Mrs. Burton and their daughter). Some visitors tried to throw a pot on Radford's wheel but with little success. Their best intentions were broken on the wheel.

My own most vivid memory of visitors is that of C. P. Scott of the *Manchester Guardian*, seated on my stool and plying me with questions. It was at the time when the lead poisoning agitation was afoot, and the Departmental Committee was enquiring into the evils of lead poisoning among pottery workers. He came accompanied by his son-in-law, C. E. Montague, to get first-hand information on the matter. I well remember that fine head, that fine face, those clear penetrating eyes that seemed to look right through me. I remember, too, the rapidity with which his mind worked. I was amazed at the rapid bombardment of questions. Hardly had an answer left my lips when 'bang' came another.

Another visitor was Sir Ernest Hatch, the chairman of the Committee. There came also H. H. S. Cunynghame, C.B., a distinguished civil servant from the Board of Trade. He was keenly interested in other aspects as well as the poisoning agitation. He tried his hand at Lustre painting whilst seated at Forsyth's wheel. He made a better job of it than did many others, although when he looked at it before it was fired his comment was 'A poor thing but mine own'. Nevertheless, it was quite an interesting design, for this cultured and accomplished man had a natural ability in art and might have been a great artist in any medium.

Another interesting personality who tried his hand was Francis Dodd, the Royal Academician, who was an old friend of the Burtons, but he made a sad mess of it from a design point of view. Accomplished portrait painter that he undoubtedly was, he was unsuitable as a pottery-designer. However, his buoyant personality saved the situation and he seemed quite satisfied with his effort.

Any record of the presence of visitors would be incomplete if it did not mention the visits of the proprietors and their families. There is no need to say anything here regarding their presence on business matters except to say that Mr. Lawrence Pilkington, in his capacity as Chairman of the Company, made regular weekly visits to the works, sometimes accompanied by his wife and daughters. He took a very keen interest in the artistic quality of the production. One received the impression of a fine type of English gentleman; tall, upright, and good-looking. He was an accomplished musician and a poet, as well as a competent business man. One who knew him well has written that for her 'he represents the finest flower of Manchester's Edwardian civilisation'. Mr. Charles Pilkington, his brother, was not so frequent a visitor but, from time to time, he came with his wife and their sons.

It is pleasant to recall that they were like the old-time patrons, when men of culture, position and wealth fostered the arts of painters, sculptors, silversmiths, and potters too. It was patronage without patronising. The nineteenth century saw its decline and the twentieth, with its high taxes and death duties, has seen its almost complete disappearance. It is fortunate that this element in the Pilkington family survived the rigours of this materialistic age and expended itself in linking art with twentieth century industry.

In this period, lustre-painting was the main occupation of the artists, but they also exercised their gifts in various other ways. They adorned pieces by modelling in relief and by the opposite method of carving. There was also clay modelling for moulds for making forms to be sprigged on the ware. Individual modelling of animals and birds occupied much of R. Joyce's time, and many plaques were made for various purposes. Much decoration by incised designs and by the *Sgraffito* method was done. The painters, though chiefly engaged on lustre, did a fair amount of painting on matt-surfaced glazes, especially in black on blue ground, and in brown and also black on vermilion ground. In technique there was constant activity exploiting the potential values of the new coloured glazes, and many fine modifications of the original colours were obtained. Some delightful brownish effects were obtained by mottling the orange-vermilion with other colours. The brilliant blue was altered in several ways, the most successful being the highly popular *Kingfisher* blue. Other varieties of transmutation glazes were also produced.

In this rush of activity the importance of maintaining quality was ever present. Joseph Burton, who was an unerring judge of pottery quality, used to speak of 'Quality with a capital "Q" ', to emphasize its importance. Every technician, every craftsman, every artist—in fact, everyone whose work influenced quality—was made well aware that it mattered. It played its part along with the ware's other excellencies in spreading its fame in many lands to bring wondering crowds to exhibitions in Paris, Milan, Brussels, Ghent, London and elsewhere. Many fine pieces have never been seen by the public, for fame brought buyers from far and near to purchase them on the spot.

A sad disaster occurred at one exhibition. On the 14th of August 1910, the whole of the British Section of the Brussels Exhibition was destroyed by fire. The financial loss was estimated at £2,000,000. But far more serious than the money loss was the loss of precious irreplaceable treasures. Among the things destroyed were choice examples of English antique furniture and many *objets d'art* from the Victoria and Albert Museum. Bernard Moore (the greatest experimental potter of his time) lost many of his unique experimental pieces, and Pilkingtons lost some very fine examples of their Lancastrian ware.

It happened that at the time of the fire, Mr. Sheppard, the firm's London area manager was on holiday in Belgium. He received a telegram from Mr. Burton asking for a full report of the firm's losses. He hastened to the scene. All that remained of the Pottery Section of the exhibition was a huge mound of rubbish, about ten feet high. He purchased a rake and raked about the heap. Coming across some broken bits of Lancastrian pottery he diligently searched the neighbourhood of these fragments. Eventually, he found half a dozen small Chinese-shape green ink-bottles, with embossed animals on the sides; they were the sole survivors—their smallness had saved them from destruction.

All other sections of the exhibition escaped the fire, and the Belgian authorities appealed to the British exhibitors to send other exhibits. They responded without delay. The new British Section was opened by the King of the Belgians on the 19th of September 1910.

Along with his report, Mr. Sheppard sent some newspapers containing photographs of the ruined buildings showing the bent and twisted steelwork. These provided a *motif* for Gordon Forsyth which he developed in the grand manner. He painted a large vase with leaping, surging, swirling tongues of lurid flame licking the distorted girders. It was an exceptionally fine piece of lustre ware, superb with the glow of fires and flames of gorgeous colour. The Belgian authorities expressed their high appreciation in a letter of thanks to the firm. I am told that immediately it was unpacked on its arrival, it was ear-marked for the city, but enquiries of the museum officials at Brussels have failed to locate it, though they have two other pieces of Lancastrian pottery: one the work of W. S. Mycock and the other by Miss Rodgers.

It will not have escaped the reader's notice that nothing has been said so far about the *tiles* which formed more than 90% of the firm's productions. Though the firm has a fine record of achievement in that branch of pottery manufacture—a record of which they are justly proud—an account of it here would not add to the value of this book. However, it is appropriate, whilst writing about art matters and particularly of Gordon Forsyth's activities, to mention two items which show that art was applied to tiles as well as to pots.

Undoubtedly the finest example of this type of work is the group of five large panels which lined the staircase walls leading to the Ceramic Gallery in Liverpool Museum. Each of the panels represents the contribution of a nation of antiquity to the development of the potter's art, and thus illustrates the great styles of historic pottery: Babylonian, Greek, Roman, Chinese and Persian. All were designed and painted by Forsyth. They therefore show his conception of historic pottery and his ability to translate ideas into material form. They show, too, his craftsmanship, for the tiles are coated with alkaline glaze, which is a very difficult medium for artists because of the brilliance and purity of the colours.

Each panel is 18 feet high and 9 feet wide. Tiles 8 inches square are used for the scenic portion, with narrower tiles for the borders. All of them are plastic-made and slip-faced, painted in underglaze colours, and coated with alkaline glaze. The one representing the contribution of Persian potters is thus executed in their own technique. It is a veritable *chef d'ouvre* (coloured prints of it exist).

During World War II, the Liverpool Museum was heavily bombed and much of the contents completely destroyed. The building in the vicinity of these panels suffered very severe damage. It is roofless, but the walls bearing these panels are, fortunately, still standing. The panels were protected by boarding and appear to be practically undamaged. Through the courtesy of Mr. J. H. Iliffe, O.B.E., M.A., the Director of the City of Liverpool Public Museums, a few of the boards were temporarily loosened that I might inspect a little of the tiling. It was a joy to see the brilliant colours and to find that the glaze has withstood the rigours of our climate and the damp and corrosive atmosphere of an industrial city, though only protected by thin wooden boards*. Three of these boarded panels are faintly seen beyond the pillars on the upper storey, shown on Plate 19.

Another very fine example of the same kind of tiling was the tiling of the bathrooms of the ill-fated *S.S. Titanic*. These were painted by Forsyth from designs by the ship's architect.

Thus, for ten years, success followed success. In 1913 His Majesty King George V was graciously pleased to confer upon the ware the title 'Royal' and henceforth it is known as ROYAL LANCASTRIAN POTTERY. Then the brilliance of noonday became overcast with threatening war clouds. The war deprived the firm of the services of many, including C. E. Cundall and Gordon M. Forsyth. A further shadow came in 1915 with the retirement of William Burton. Later, Charles Cundall removed to London, preferring picture and portrait painting, and in 1920 Gordon Forsyth left to become Superintendent of Art Instruction at the City of Stoke-on-Trent Schools of Art.

These important men were not replaced. There was no renewal of strength as was the case at Ching-te-Chen during the reign of the Emperor K'ang-hsi (1662-1722), when Ts'ang Yung-hsuan became director. To his period is attributed the revival of many old effects in coloured glazes and the invention of new effects as well. 'They that renew their strength mount up with wings as eagles; they run and are not weary.'

It was inevitable that a decline would set in, for no firm can sustain itself solely on the laurels of the past. The works ceased to

---

* We owe the knowledge that these panels are safe to the persistent enquiries of an elderly Liverpool lady, Miss Susan Firth, daughter of the potter J. T. Firth of Kirkby Lonsdale, mentioned in Chapter 2. The Liverpool civic authorities had no knowledge of them and suggested that they had been dumped somewhere with other rubbish.

be a magnet drawing scientists, artists, and other cultured people to its studios. Moreover, the firm was without a trained works chemist for sixteen years; consequently nothing outstandingly new in glazes was produced in those years. Even some earlier discoveries were not exploited.

A step in the right direction was made when, in November 1927, Arthur Chambers, son of John Chambers, the first designer of the firm, was engaged as works chemist, a position which he held for the next eleven years. Between my time and his the works had grown considerably, and so had the volume of production, with the result that the day-to-day duties of the works chemist in controlling the quality of the bodies, glazes, and colours, and in supervising the increasing number of 'trials' needed to cope with the growing number of problems of production left him little time for experimental work of the kind that I had the good fortune to have time for, and so systematic exploratory research was practically non-existent in his time. In one matter, however, he rendered conspicuous service. In the winter of 1927 the growing trade in matt glazed tiles and slabs for fireplace surrounds received an impetus from the discovery that titanium oxide, in the form of the mineral rutile, had the peculiar property of inducing a mottled colour-effect in these matt glazes. All the makers of fireplace surrounds were exploiting the idea. Joseph Burton called Arthur Chambers' attention to this development and asked him to see what he could do in the matter. He succeeded in producing excellent self-mottling glazes, to which the name 'Cunian' (from Mancunian) was given. They were largely used both on tiles and pottery. Some fine examples were exhibited at a British Industries Fair along with speckled matt glazed and Lapis wares.

The decline in Royal Lancastrian Pottery was checked in 1928 by the appearance of an entirely new style of decoration, to which the name 'Lapis Ware'* was given, because in some respects it is

* See Chapter 7.

49

reminiscent of stoneware, although the colours and glazes are richer in quality than those usually associated with stoneware. This new style of decoration was discovered by making a complete departure from traditional methods; in fact, the method adopted was exactly the reverse of the way things are generally done.

Usually the potter compounds his colours and glazes in such a way that the chemical interaction between them is at the minimum in order that the decoration shall remain fixed and definite and the colours firm and solid. Precision of outline and stability of colour are precious qualities in some styles of decoration. The Persian and Turkish potters were masters in the art of painting pottery with sharp outlines and still colours, even when relatively thick transparent glazes were to be fused over them.

Joseph Burton went in the opposite direction. He prepared a range of underglaze colours which would react very considerably with the overlying glaze and stain it. He used matt glazes because their peculiar qualities of sluggish fusibility, of opacity where thick and transparency where thin, and the soft velvety feel of the surface eminently fitted them for the new procedure. It was a bold venture, for to most people it would seem senseless to paint a pot with colour and then cover it with an opaque glaze. Fortune favoured the brave and amply rewarded him with a new distinctive kind of pottery which instantly won favour from a discerning public.

The coming of Lapis Ware brought a breath of new life into the declining industry, but it was not sufficient to ward off the approaching end, for not long after it appeared the trade depression of the early nineteen-thirties set in. The middle classes, who had been the main purchasers of the new ware, had difficulty in making ends meet and sales fell seriously. Dealers urged the firm to produce something cheaper, but their appeals were steadfastly declined, since cheapening could only be done at the expense of quality.

Another contributory factor was the failing health of Joseph

Burton. He died in December 1934. For a few years he had been a sick man. He was succeeded by his son David who for several years had acted as assistant manager and had become well acquainted with management matters. Unfortunately his health also failed.

Lacking inspiration and driving force, amid adverse economic circumstances, and with a sick man in charge, the manufacture naturally became financially unjustifiable. The directors were in the unenviable position of having to decide whether to continue or bend to the insistent pressure of events. They chose the latter and in September 1937, decided to cease manufacture. In the following month the potter's wheel ceased to revolve and the presser laid aside his moulds. Pottery in the biscuit state continued to be glazed until the following March when the last glazing kiln was fired. Pieces fired in that last glazing kiln are marked on the base 'March 1938'.

Thus ended Chapter 1 of Royal Lancastrian Pottery and with it a glorious episode in the story of English decorative pottery. (Ten years later manufacture was resumed on a small scale with new men and new ideas. The name of the ware remains the same, but the marks and the style are different.)

Summarised, Royal Lancastrian Pottery advanced the 'Art of the Potter' more than any other English pottery ever did and did it in the short space of a third of a century. It gave a richer content of beauty to this many-centuries-old craft by adding new varieties and creating new means for decoration by artists.

The new colours and surfaces of its glazes and the wonderful opalescent and crystalline effects in the glazes brought to light unsuspected riches of colour, surface, and appearance. By these means the domain of pottery unadorned by artists was considerably enlarged and at the same time its scope as a medium for applied art was also enlarged, for its matt surface glaze proved to be eminently suitable as a ground upon which artists could ply their skill. And other potters, following in the wake of Pilkingtons, evolved

51

smoother surfaces capable of receiving more delicate designs.

Lancastrian Lustre pottery preserved an ancient art and added to its glories both technically and artistically. The first by demonstrating that the process was applicable to many other types of glazes besides the alkaline glazes of the Persians and the tin enamel glazes of the Spanish and Italian potters, and by demonstrating that the elusive process of its production could be controlled to a far higher degree than was thought possible. The mastery of the technique, though very far from being absolute, was advanced so far that a relatively high proportion of successful pieces was obtained. It was these factors of glaze composition, glaze colour, and control of technique which, united with painted decoration of the highest order, yielded the abundance of superb examples which spread its fame in many lands.

The new glazes were additions to existing practice and the iridescent lustre was the enrichment of an old technique, but Lapis Ware is a child of this century having neither progenitor nor roots in the past. It was a new, original and novel way of decorating pottery by harmoniously blending coloured design and delicately tinted velvety glaze so as to produce a soft and soothing effect. It arose in an understanding mind which was rich in knowledge of glaze peculiarities and characteristics. Born inside the craft, owing nothing to external stimulus nor to existing practices, it is essentially a product of the potter, and yet it is unique, which is indeed truly remarkable.

The contribution of Royal Lancastrian Pottery to the progress of ceramics did not stop with the production of the above-mentioned features. Its influence has continued ever since, for it set a fashion and stimulated other potters to like endeavours. It awakened potters and lovers of pottery to a livelier sense of the value of colour, and to a faith in the possibility of other wondrous riches yet to be revealed.

52

SECTION

2

Wonderful Discoveries

THE INTENSE EFFORT put forth in achieving the great successes described in the preceding chapters is not obvious in the reading of the story, and it would not be surprising if some readers concluded that success just fell into the firm's lap through sheer good fortune.

For instance, Chapter 2 tells of an accidental discovery of a new glaze possessing extraordinary qualities, some of which it describes, but it tells nothing of the immense effort made during the five months immediately following its discovery. Again, Chapter 3 tells of the revival of iridescent lustre painting and describes some of the masterpieces that were produced, but no reader would gather from that chapter the immense difficulty of the process and the disappointments and discouragements that have been the lot of all who have attempted its production.

Hence the necessity for a section which will tell in greater detail how the Lancastrian potters achieved their greatest successes; emphasising the parts played by fortunate discoveries, by systematic research, by perseverance in face of frequent disappointments, and the triumphant combination of fine craftsmanship, science, and artistic skill.

CHAPTER 5

Its Opalescent and Crystalline Glazes

OPALESCENT GLAZES

WHEN THE NINETEENTH CENTURY was ending, the attention of English potters was called to the desirability of using leadless glazes in order to avoid lead poisoning among their workers, and many of them made experiments to that end. Very soon it was seen that leadless glazes had a tendency to milkiness. The same thing had been noticed years before by other potters, but this milkiness was practically a new phenomenon to manufacturers of English earthenware and china, for they were accustomed to lead glazes which had good transparency. The milky appearance was regarded as a defect, as indeed it was for those wares. Apparently no one thought that the milkiness was anything but a nuisance. We ourselves had met with it early in our career, and had made some little use of it, but its possibilities as a rich decorative medium did not dawn on us until the accidental discovery mentioned in Chapter 2 occurred.

The frit mentioned in Chapter 2 was a brilliant, clear, transparent glass and apparently a homogeneous substance, but when it was ground to fine powder and applied to the surface of pottery and fired in a usual pottery glazing kiln parts of it were clouded. The cloudiness varied considerably from piece to piece and even on the same piece. Its behaviour in this respect was unpredictable and excited much curiosity. What sort of effects would it produce if applied to pottery with uneven surface where the glaze, after firing, would be uneven in thickness? What sort of results would be obtained if it were applied on coloured bodies? What would happen if colouring oxides or other substances were added to it? etc. Trials were at once put in hand.

In the five months from October 1903 to March 1904 no fewer than 200 additions of various materials were made, and others were made later. Fifty different substances were added, including oxides, fluorides, chromates, uranates, phosphates, vanadates, arsenite, arsenates, oxalates, and aluminates in varying amounts.

Very interesting and extraordinary results were obtained. Additions of oxide of zinc and firing in the biscuit oven gave the glaze a cellular structure. Adding vanadium oxide made the glaze iridescent, and so did some vanadates and also bismuth chromate. Chromates gave variable results. Many of them gave the same colour as that given by about one-third the amount of chromium oxide, whereas manganese chromate gave the same depth of colour as manganese oxide does, and tin chromate, even with as much as 5%, gave no colour at all. The addition of cobalt aluminate gave a much more beautiful broken colour effect than did the addition of cobalt oxide. Oxide of iron could be added in quantities up to 20%, giving fine effects passing description.

With this unique frit as a basis we produced, in William Burton's words 'glazes which develop layers, streaks, or patches of opalescent, feathered, or clouded colour effects in subtle and beautiful gradations, showing striae which may be infinitely finer than they could be drawn by a painter, or may take the form of more or less opaque featherings or cloudings. The forms assumed are so subtle, and so varied, that the resultant glazes have been compared by different observers to all kinds of beautiful natural products; to finely grained and highly polished woods, to polished serpentine, agate and jasper; to the feathery moss in a running stream, and to the lightest "cirri" in the summer sky'.

Though the possibilities of this unusual glaze had only been partially explored by November 1905, sufficient had been revealed to make William Burton take the risk of launching out on the large scale manufacture of decorative pottery; a decision which was followed by immediate success.

The many novel and uncertain effects produced in this glaze were utterly unlike anything hitherto seen in pottery glazes, and plainly indicate that the glaze possesses some very peculiar properties. The additions of different colouring oxides and chromates produce results which differ from each other far more than do the results of similar additions to other glazes, and opalescence appears in odd places and at times with striking colour effects. The ordinary variations inside a kiln during firing operations are not powerful enough, of themselves, to effect such changes, nor are changes in the composition of the glaze during firing caused by 'foreign' substances dissolved from the clay body.

A possible explanation is that the glaze is far more delicately sensitive to disturbing influences than are other glazes. It may well be that when it melts during the firing process it is homogeneous and transparent but when disturbed by something it changes into a mixture of immiscible fluids of different refractivities and thus becomes opalescent. If that is so, it offers a possible explanation of the phenomena of veining. These veins are sometimes as much as 6 inches long, and no glaze would flow that distance. It may be that, just as a small crystal put into a supersaturated solution causes crystallisation to proceed through the liquid, so a 'foreign' substance entering this glaze may start a change which spreads rapidly, and if the glaze was being fired in a vertical position might, aided by a downward tendency in the glaze, spread rapidly downward without any change of position.

Plate 24 well illustrates the delicate sensitivity of this opal glaze to disturbing factors. From all the points in the design where incised lines cross each other there starts an exceedingly fine spray

20. (Above) Crystals in glaze frit.
21. (Below) Fiery crystalline glaze. Actual size.

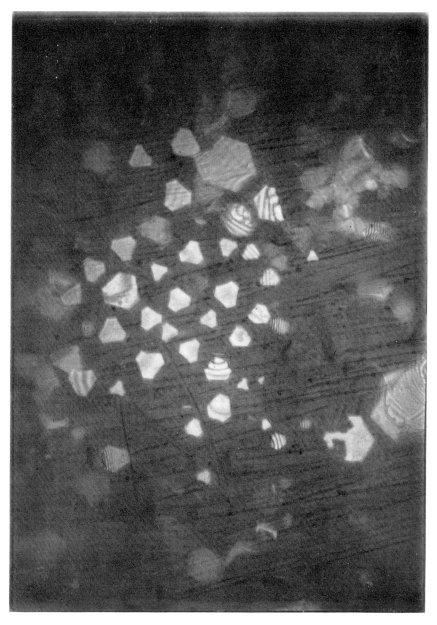

22. Fiery crystals of Plate No. 21 magnified × 210

23. A fiery crystal magnified × 700

24. Two variations of this extraordinary glaze [See page 57]. Dish is modern, disc is 1903-04.

Dish 11 in. dia., interior $2\frac{1}{2}$ in. deep. Disc 4 in. dia.   *Author's collection*

of white opalescence which falls downward with the flow of the glaze and hides the colour of the ground, thus causing the realistic and beautiful effect of water fountains. This effect is heightened by the sprays falling into a pool of pale greenish-blue liquid at the base. Possibly something at the crossings unsettled the unstable equilibrium of the glaze resulting in the formation of sprays. A closer inspection of the piece reveals another beautiful and interesting feature. The channelled incisions are seen to contain green lines, many of them varied in a way that no artist's brush could produce. Whereas the spray is white the incisions are green. Why? This is another of the mysteries of this exceptional glaze.

The dish is $11\frac{1}{2}$ inches wide and $2\frac{1}{2}$ inches deep with sloping sides. It has a very sound body, a well made shape, a skilfully drawn pattern, and a perfectly matured coloured glaze. These excellences of the potter's craft give pleasure to the beholder, but without the aid of opalescence this piece—which is now a gem—would not have been so full of interest.

CRYSTALLINE GLAZES

Many glazes within a wide range of composition are prone to crystallisation. Crystals can appear in simple silicates, in borates, in boro-silicates, as well as in very complex glaze compositions. They appear in lead glazes and in glazes free from lead; in the interior of glazes, and on the surface. Thin coats of glaze and thick masses of frit are liable to contain them. They take various forms, such as thin needles, thick needles, radiating groups of needles, spherical clusters, devitrified masses like frozen snow and surface flowers like those on a frosted window pane. There are colourless crystals and coloured ones; among the latter are brilliant shining golden specks and glittering spangles which reflect light like burnished copper.

The most striking of all the examples of the tendency to crystallise that we met with is the piece of glaze frit shown on Plate 20.

That remarkable instance resulted from a mishap. At the time when this happened it was our practice to make bulk quantities of frit in an open hearth furnace fired at a high temperature. Some of the frits were very fluid and had a strong, corrosive action on the firebrick lining. On one occasion, the molten frit corroded its way through the joints between the fireclay blocks that formed the floor of the furnace and formed pools of frit underneath. The piece illustrated is part of one of those pools. In it are seen many bunches of white crystals, spherical in shape, some being fully one inch in diameter. They are made up of peculiar individual pieces shaped something like a double-bladed canoeing paddle, and are about one inch long, with thick ends and a thin rod-like centre piece. The thick ends look like sheaths over a thin rod.

Sufficient has now been said to demonstrate the tendency of glazes to form crystals. Nevertheless, we did not find it easy to produce the radiating crystals so much desired. A measure of success attended our efforts but the results were so capricious that the experiments were finally abandoned.

Here is a brief summary of our efforts to produce glazes with radiating crystals. They were initiated by William Burton, who had been deeply impressed with those he had seen at the Paris exhibition of 1900. Soon after his return he set me on the task, followed my efforts with keen interest, and made suggestions from time to time. Our chief method was the saturation of glazes of various kinds with zinc oxide. One of the first difficulties encountered which stayed with us for the whole time we were on the work, was the capricious character of the results. Glaze compositions which sometimes yielded good results often failed when repeated. This was a plain indication that other factors were operative besides glaze composition. Firing temperature had a great influence and so had rate of cooling. The best results were obtained from firing the glazed pieces in the biscuit oven. Some successful results were obtained with double glazing. A glaze rich in zinc oxide was first applied and fired. On the top of this another glaze was put and again fired. When the first coat contained a little oxide of titanium along with the zinc oxide and the second coat was a simple soda-zinc silicate some very good results were obtained, especially when they were fired in the biscuit oven. Altogether about a thousand experiments were made. Successful pieces were exhibited at the 1904 exhibition. The manufacture ceased because of the continued uncertainty of the results.

Our successes were with the other type of crystalline glazes. The production of the glazes with glittering specks and spangles presented no difficulty. Very early in the firm's existence Joseph Burton produced his first glaze of this type by saturating a rich lead glaze with chromate of iron. Later he produced a similar one using chromate of copper. These crystalline glazes were very similar to the glazes produced some years earlier at the Rookwood pottery in U.S.A., which have been likened to 'Sparkles in the stone Aventurine'. Joseph Burton gave the name 'Sunstone' to his glaze. Later, similar glittering specks and spangles were obtained by the use of sodium uranate. Some years later small golden glittering specks were produced by saturating a rich lead glaze with oxide of iron. These were best displayed if the glaze was applied on a red body.

Earlier in this Chapter it is suggested that opalescence in glazes may be due to the separation of a silicate out of a mixture of silicates in such a way that it becomes visible. The crystals that separate out during the cooling of a glaze must be regarded as analogous, since their shape points to their being silicates formed in the glaze.

Our greatest success commenced in 1903 with crystals in glazes obtained by adding oxide of iron to the glaze frit from which the opalescent glazes were produced, doubtless because its sensitivity to internal stresses operating during firing and cooling is exceptionally acute.

59

The glaze is of a bright yellow colour, shot through and through with lines, groups, or patches of brilliant golden crystals. The crystals are much larger than the sunstone crystals and are so brilliant that they make the vase or piece of pottery on which they are applied shine like burnished copper. They are developed in their full perfection and brilliance when fired at a temperature of about 1,000°C. On firing harder the crystals become much smaller and change to a beautiful purple.

These bright, copper-coloured glazes are obtained if a white body is used. If a coloured body is used the colour and size of the crystals change, and the whole piece is very different. Another variety of glaze effect is obtained when still more oxide is used in the glaze, for this causes a separation of black particles in and on the surface of the glaze, making a charming black mottling on a dull reddish copper-coloured glaze.

Altogether, a varied assortment of intensely interesting effects was obtained. They are interesting, not only in colour and variety, but also in the shape of their crystals. The three plates Nos. 21, 22, 23, provide a fascinating study in crystallisation.

CHAPTER 6

New Coloured Glazes

The colouring of pottery glazes is quite a simple matter. All that is necessary is the addition of small amounts of colouring substances to the glaze mixture. Though it is as simple as that the potter is restricted in the colours he can produce, for he has only about a dozen substances that will withstand the fierce heat of his kilns. He is not so fortunate as the textile dyer who has five thousand dyes at his service. The principal colouring substances used by the potter are metallic oxides; those most used being the oxides of manganese for teapot brown, iron for brownish yellows, copper for greens, and cobalt for blues. The oxides of chromium, uranium, antimony and a few others are occasionally used and also the chromates of iron and copper.

The potter rings the changes with these materials by adding different amounts, by using mixtures, by using glazes of different composition, by firing at different temperatures, and, in a few instances, by changing the composition of his kiln atmosphere.

In a lead glaze such as that used on wall and fireplace tiles a thousand hues can be obtained by using only the first four oxides mentioned.

For pinks and crimsons a pigment is prepared by intimately mixing calcium carbonate, flint, and a small amount of chromium oxide or other chromium compound and firing the mixture at a high temperature. About 10% of the pigment is added to a glaze of suitable composition for a deep crimson colour.

Coloured glazes were a prominent feature of Royal Lancastrian

61

Pottery throughout the whole period of its manufacture and they made a notable contribution to its fame. Among them were many fine examples of the usual type of coloured glazes, for the works had had ten years experience in making many such glazes used by them on wall and fireplace tiles. In addition to these were some new colours of exceptional beauty which had never been seen previously in the long history of ceramics. There was a new and brilliant ultramarine blue and a new richly coloured orange glaze obtained by the use of uranium. Many modifications of these two new glazes were made making them even more attractive, especially the one known as Orange-Vermilion, which became famous in many lands. Some of the ware had choice shades of deep red obtained by firing in a reducing atmosphere glaze containing a small amount of oxide of copper. The experiments which produced these results are described herein. There is also an account of a most extraordinary glaze which gave, from the same colouring oxide, both sky blue and leaf green when fired in identical conditions, which is certainly unique.

ULTRAMARINE BLUE

This, the first of the new colours, was discovered in 1903. It was an exceedingly vivid blue glaze unlike any blue hitherto seen in pottery glaze.

To understand fully how this unique blue was discovered readers should refer to Chapter 13, particularly to the part dealing with the Periodicity of the Elements, for it is explained there how it comes about that one material may sometimes be substituted for another. It was one such substitution—that of oxide of zinc (ZnO) for lime (CaO) in the composition of an eggshell glaze—that provided the glaze which yielded this exceptional colour with oxide of cobalt.

Never having previously seen a glaze of this composition I naturally sought to find its colour developing powers. Trials were made, sent to the kiln and, as usual, the matter passed out of my mind.

Some days afterwards when the trials came out of the kiln they were laid out on my bench by my assistant as was customarily done, to await my arrival.

Imagine my astonishment at seeing this most exceptional colour there. It was miles ahead of the best blue glaze we then had. I was thrilled and immediately hastened to find Joseph Burton. I took with me a tile of this new colour and one of our previous best blue. The experience must have thrown me temporarily off my balance, for I remember greeting him with some such absurdity as 'A thing of beauty is a joy for ever; if it ceases to be a joy, does it cease to be a thing of beauty?' 'What do you mean,' he said. Showing him the earlier blue I said 'This used to please us, but what of this?' showing him the new one. 'What is this' he asked; evidently astonished with its brilliance. The rapture of that great moment is an abiding memory. It was indeed one of life's highlights.

The colour of this ultramarine blue glaze is of exceptional brilliance and purity. So pure and vivid is its colour that it attracts attention to itself and thereby diminishes its usefulness. When it made its first public appearance along with the other coloured glazes at the exhibition of 1904 it was described by an onlooker as 'a queer poisonous blue which seemed to sing out above the others'. The accuracy of that description was demonstrated by purchasers finding that wherever it was placed in a room it put all other pottery out of key. It could find no resting place and sales soon ceased.

A modified version of it, known by various names but chiefly as Kingfisher Blue, made by lightly speckling it with a bright green, proved to be very popular, especially in Australia. Why in Australia? Because the clear atmosphere and brilliant sunshine prevalent there provide more favourable conditions than our atmosphere does. The full glory of this most beautiful colour is seen only when brilliant sunshine falls directly upon it. On dull days our smoke-laden atmosphere hides its beauty. In the clear atmosphere and brilliant sunshine of the Australian scene the colour is seen in its full glory.

URANIUM GLAZES

The date when uranium glaze was first produced at Clifton Junction is not known, for the earliest records have not been kept. Fortunately, existing records show that a uranium sunstone glaze was in use in 1902. It had a pleasant light brown colour and a semi-matt surface. Examination of it with a lens revealed innumerable small golden crystals evenly distributed throughout the glaze. Associated with these crystals, and also evenly distributed, are specks of a darker brown of a slightly redder hue.

Using a little less uranium, so that the glaze would not be fully saturated, a variety of effects resulted. Some pieces had a rich yellow glaze, devoid of crystals, but speckled reddish brown all over, as if some granules had been dusted on to it. Other pieces, generally the larger ones, had areas of transparent yellow and areas that were identical to the sunstone glaze above described. Other parts of the same piece might be mottled, and if the shape facilitated a downward flow of the glaze, the mottling would show a dragged effect. The amount and distribution of these peculiarities varied from piece to piece, making this 'Mottled Sunstone' an attractive style of decoration.

My note book of 13th August 1904, records that uranium sunstone glaze was coming out bad, being ruckled and of an unpleasant colour. On examining the glaze slip I found that it had separated into two parts, the lower portion having *set*. The upper portion, after being separated from the remainder, was stirred up and tiles marked 'A' were dipped in it. Similarly tiles marked 'B' were dipped in the stirred up bottom layer. Finally, the two lots were mixed together and tiles marked 'C' were dipped in the mixture.

After firing the results were:

A. Glaze is all ruckled and a nasty colour.

B. An exceptionally fine amber coloured glaze. The finest I have ever seen. Glaze quality is simply perfect.

C. The usual sunstone effect.

1. ULTRAMARINE BLUE   Discovered 1903
Height $5\frac{1}{4}$ ins.   *Author's Collection*
'A queer poisonous blue'
For particulars of its discovery see Page 62

2. URANIUM ORANGE
Height 13¼ in.   *Author's Collection*
The first Uranium Orange ever made in the world
For particulars of its chance discovery see Page 64

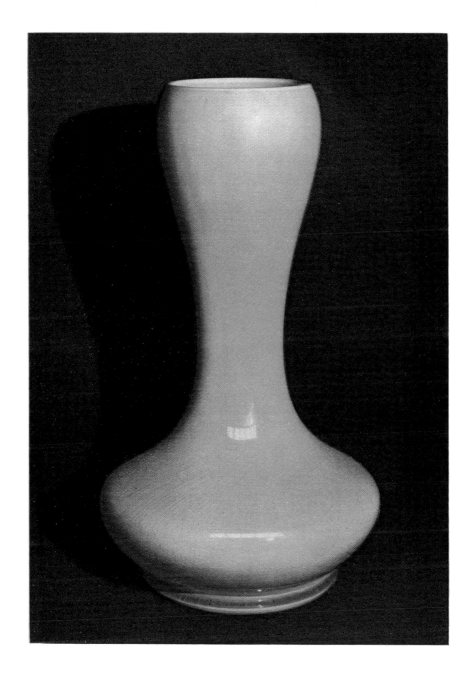

5. KINGFISHER BLUE
Height $7\frac{1}{4}$ in. *Author's Collection*
A modification of the Ultramarine Blue
An exceptional colour since its real beauty is seen
  only when direct sunlight falls upon it
See Page 63

4. ORANGE-VERMILION
Height 10½ in.   *Author's Collection*
A natural development of the Uranium Orange
See Page 65

(The description of the colour as amber is incorrect. The colour was by far the purest, richest, and most beautiful orange glaze we had ever seen, and great was our exultation.)

Acting on the assumption that the bottom layer contained a greater proportion of the heavier constituents of the glaze than did the upper, a glaze was made containing a high proportion of lead frit. It proved satisfactory in every respect, giving the rich orange glaze of which Joseph Burton was speaking when, at the Royal Society of Arts on 15th January 1930, he said that this was the first uranium orange glaze made in the world. Coming at the moment when we were launching on a new career, hoping to impress the public by our freshness, it was a fortunate and welcome addition to our list of coloured glazes.

This signal success beckoned one to new fields of adventure. It certainly stimulated further search. Assiduous efforts were made to find what lay beyond. These were crowned with success when, eighteen months later, they culminated in the world famous *Orange-Vermilion* glaze.

Most of the experiments consisted of additions of uranium— either as the black oxide, or as sodium uranate or lead uranate—to lead glazes. Beginning with a glaze containing 25% of lead oxide, the experiments continued by regular stages to one with a very high content of lead. Lead uranate proved to be more soluble in these glazes than sodium uranate. After a certain depth of colour had been reached with lead uranate further additions made very little difference in shade, and there were no indications that there was any saturation point. On the other hand, additions of sodium uranate reached a point when spangles and glittering crystals separated out in cooling. The glazes tended to give black separations, especially when the black oxide of uranium was used.

With a frit compounded only of red lead, china clay and flint, a beautiful, opaque, tangerine glaze was produced by adding sodium uranate. In a different type of highly leaded glaze a most unusual result appeared on one occasion. Sodium uranate was added to the glaze in amount exceeding the maximum for a transparent glaze. Tiles were glazed with this and fired in the ordinary way in the majolica glaze kiln. After firing, some of the tiles had an almost solid red skin, but most of them were dark brown, almost black. Spread about their surface were many brilliant red circular crystalline patches. The dark brown was due to an insoluble substance floating on the surface of a lighter coloured glaze.

These frequent appearances of novel and unexpected effects intensified our interest in the work. Naturally, the experiments were continued with zest. A succession of brilliant beautiful glazes rejoiced our hearts. Here are some of the descriptive notes made at the time. They are taken from my note book: 'broken red and gold mottle'; 'almost solid red'; 'yellow with golden spangles'; 'red and gold broken glaze'; 'beautiful rich orange glaze flecked with red and containing innumerable small golden spangles'.

The glaze finally selected was named ORANGE-VERMILION. Its appearance created quite a sensation, and attracted buyers from all over the world. It was imitated in many lands. The brilliance of the colour called forth modifications in addition to those given by the vermilion separations. These were obtained by speckling and splashing with dark brown or black and simple dark brushwork, all of which gave an added charm to an already lovely ware. An all-over stippled brown variety was much admired.

ROUGE FLAMBÉ GLAZES

The term 'flambé' has strayed so far from its original meaning that to many people it denotes all kinds of red glazes that are stained with copper oxide and fired in a reducing atmosphere. The variegated colour of the finest Chinese examples are classed by them with the uniform blood red of Messrs. Doulton as one and the same thing.

Pilkingtons' flambé was unlike both of them. Though it varied from kiln to kiln, from piece to piece and sometimes from front to back, it seldom had the broken variegated colour of the Chinese product. It was nearer to the Doulton style. The successful production of a glaze with the same uniform blood red colour time after time is a technical achievement of the highest order, and the person who devised the process merits the thanks of all who take delight in technically perfect coloured glazes. Lancastrian flambé had charming pottery colour varying from pale strawberry and cherry to the deepest blood red, occasionally accompanied with a lustrous radiance or a burnished metallic reflection.

William Burton was enamoured of Chinese flambé. He often spoke of its glories, and wrote effusively about it. He was impressed with Bernard Moore's achievements, and with the exhibits of flambé at the Paris exhibition of 1900. I am unable to trace how early we began experiments for it, but the records show that in the period from April 1901 to May 1904, many were made, and all of them were suggested by William Burton. A summary of them is given below; they indicate that he was feeling his way over strange ground.

Almost all the glazes used in these early experiments were leadless glazes. All contained a small amount of copper oxide, sometimes accompanied by small amounts of such other materials as the oxides of iron, tin, and cobalt, magnesium or aluminium dust and reduced iron. The addition of barium carbonate was also tried. Frequently the pieces were supported over shallow trays containing a few grams of a mixture of copper and lead acetates.

The pieces were usually fired in saggars in an ordinary glost oven and sometimes in a muffle kiln. The saggars were double walled with the intervening space filled with a mixture of rice carbon and granular flint to produce a reducing atmosphere and their tops were covered with lids. Later, carbon-impregnated saggars, produced by saturating the walls and base with concentrated sugar solution, were used.

At times both methods gave some really fine results, especially when glazes containing a little reduced iron or tin oxide were used and the pieces were supported over mixed acetates of copper and lead.

Experiments on these lines were discontinued in May 1904, and do not appear to have been resumed until January 1906, when a new muffle kiln was built. This was constructed for lustre firing and was also used for flambé. To correct a misapprehension that is abroad it should be stated that all Royal Lancastrian Rouge Flambé had low-temperature glaze.

DUAL COLOURED NICKEL GLAZE

It is said that an old potter advised his son never to use nickel in making his colours. Dr. Mellor used to say that that advice, even if too general, is essentially sound, for most of the nickel browns, drabs, fawns, and buff colours can be produced by other more reliable means.

The experiences of potters with nickel oxide have differed considerably. Seger found that it gave dirty greens when used as underglaze colour. We found that it yielded a variety of colours. In a lime matt glaze it gave dull browns and dull greens according to the amount added. With a magnesia matt glaze increasing the amount of nickel made little difference, for the addition of so large an amount as 20% gave only a light drab colour. With a zinc matt glaze it gave greyish blues. Those experiments were made in 1903. In 1904 it gave yellow deepening to brown in an alkaline boro-silicate glaze. In 1907, we found on making some nickel aluminate, that it was a beautiful sky blue. In 1909 we had an unexpected result, for on adding nickel carbonate and zinc oxide together to an alkaline boro-silicate glaze it gave bright blue crystals in a brown glaze.

Scientific ceramic literature of later days contains many references to the strange behaviour of nickel in glazes. To quote Dr.

Mellor, 'These nickel colours are unstable and unreliable. They develop variations of tint when fired under all three types of glazes—raw lead, fritted lead, and leadless glazes. These observations make it very doubtful if anything can be done with nickel oxide until some new mode of treatment is discovered.'

It has fallen to our lot to get the upper hand of this capricious colorant. In April 1910, on adding gradually increasing amounts of nickel oxide to a matt glaze containing both oxides of zinc and tin we found that so small an amount as $0\cdot5\%$ gave a surprisingly strong sky blue, and $3\text{-}5\%$ gave a quiet leaf green. These results were not flukes, for much architectural faience was glazed with this green. Moreover, Messrs. Pilkington have recently kindly repeated the experiments for me and they have yielded precisely the same results. The two colours can be seen on a bowl in the Hanley Museum at Stoke-on-Trent.

This is a discovery of historic importance. Ever since man began to coat his pottery with coloured glazes he has had only five ways by which he could change the colour.

1. By changing the colorant used. Manganese oxide in an earthenware lead glaze gives a teapot brown. Cobalt oxide in a similar glaze gives blues.
2. By using mixtures of colorants.
3. By changing the composition of the glaze. Manganese oxide which gives a teapot brown in an earthenware glaze gives an amethyst purple in an alkaline glaze, and copper oxide which gives green in an earthenware glaze gives a turquoise blue in an alkaline glaze.
4. By changing the firing temperature. The turquoise blue given by copper oxide in an alkaline glaze changes to green on harder firing.
5. By changing the composition and character of the kiln atmosphere. The well-known *Rouge Flambé* colour is a striking example of this. A small amount of copper oxide

in a glaze fired in an oxidising atmosphere gives a pale bluish green, but if fired in a reducing atmosphere gives a deep blood red.

These five methods were all the potter had, though he could, of course, combine methods. For instance, uranium oxide in a lead glaze and fired at a moderate heat gives yellow, but if added to a felspathic glaze and fired at the great heat of hard paste porcelain firing it gives black.

This two-in-one nickel glaze, discovered in 1910, differs from all others. The colour change is not brought about by any of the five methods hitherto used. Summarising the methods:

1. There is no change of colorant. Nickel oxide is used in both cases.
2. There is no mixture of colorants. Only one is used in both cases.
3. There is no change of glaze. The same glaze is used in both cases.
4. There is no change of firing temperature, for both are fired together.
5. There is no change of kiln atmosphere, for both are fired together.

The only change is in the amount of colorant added. *This is a new phenomenon. It is another milestone on the road that pottery travels.*

70

CHAPTER 7

Lapis Ware

LAPIS is the name given to an entirely new style of pottery which came into being in 1928 and continued to be made until the manufacture of Royal Lancastrian Pottery ceased in 1938. It differs from all other kinds of pottery in the manner of its production and the character of its decoration. Like much other decorated pottery it is painted by artist's brush, but in a way not known to potters and artists until Pilkingtons introduced it in 1928. Previously, artists had only three ways of painting their designs on pottery. They could (1) paint on pottery which was not to be glazed, (2) on pottery which would be coated with a transparent glaze afterwards, or (3) on the surface of already glazed pottery. No other method was known. Lapis decoration differs from all others in that painters designs are in the *interior* of the glaze and throughout its thickness. This new method gives the ware an indefinable charm not possessed by any other class of pottery.

For this new method of painting, specially compounded pigments and a glaze with unusual characteristics are needed. The pigment is applied in the same way that underglaze colours are ordinarily applied, i.e., on the pot in its biscuit (once fired) state, and is then coated with the glaze mixture. The compositions of both pigment and glaze are such that disagreement and strife occur during the firing, with consequent change and upheaval. The pigment softens and merges with the glaze, some of it reaches the surface in a speckly condition and some of it dissolves but does not spread too far in the surrounding glaze. In consequence, however sharply

71

defined a design may be when painted, the subsequent fusion of the glaze changes its character considerably by mottling its colour and blurring its edges. This discovery of a way to modify an artist's painted design by speckling and mottling it, and at the same time softening its outlines yet preserving the design as a whole has provided artists with a new and wider field in which to display their talents.

Pilkingtons chose for the new ware the name LAPIS because, they said, it is reminiscent of stoneware in some respects, and also reminiscent of Lapis Lazuli. Stoneware is the name given to such a great variety of clay products that it has little meaning until it is more sharply defined. Lapis ware has nothing in common with many of them except that it, like them, is made from clay. It has nothing in common, for instance, with the excellent domestic culinary ware made of a hard, compact, close grained, impervious clay body, nor with the chemical stoneware vessels used for storing corrosive liquids, nor with the common drain pipes used by the builder. Narrowing the term down to the type of pottery about which many pottery books are written, Lapis ware has little similarity with the ware imported from the Rhineland in the sixteenth and seventeenth centuries, or with the unglazed red pottery, the polished black basalt figures, the coloured jasper, the Parian busts, and the salt glazed wares of the eighteenth century. What then likens it to stoneware?

As a potter, stoneware, to me, is one of the many varieties of pottery located between the rude, easy-fired crocks of our forefathers and the fine chinaware of our modern factories. The clay is more carefully selected and better prepared and harder fired than the former, yet not so carefully selected and blended nor so highly purified as the latter. Its glaze is more complex than the galena glaze of the former, but not so carefully and elaborately compounded as the latter. Peasant pottery is of the earth, earthy. Fine chinaware is of the laboratory, fragile, pure and undefiled.

72

Stoneware embodies strength, stability, and permanence and, abhorring the shine of the polisher, offers an outward surface more akin to that of unpolished marble. Stoneware has no place for delicacy, fragility, high gloss, glaring colour, or artist's finesse, for they convey a sense of instability. It has solidity, weight, appropriate form and surface, sober colour and restrained decoration, for they signify the strength, quietness and permanence of the rocks. Lapis ware at its best possesses these qualities.

From whence does Lapis get her charm? From two sources; one artistic and the other technical. The unusual character of the colouring and the style of decoration contribute and so do the internal peculiarities of the glaze. When compared with other dull and semi-dull glazes, subtle differences of appearance, feel, and colour are recognised.

Many influences are at work during the firing of Lapis glaze. Its composition causes sluggish fusibility, and viscous mobility results when the glaze is fused. Moreover, the glaze possesses a high degree of surface tension and thereby tends to curl inwards upon itself. When such a glaze is applied to pottery in the biscuit state, its water is absorbed by the porous biscuit. The glaze powder dries and shrinks and cracks appear and it is from the edges of these cracks the glaze curls inwardly during the firing process. Plate 38 shows an extreme example of shrinking and consequent curling. Generally the glaze melts sufficiently for the parts to flow together and heal the cracks. With the aid of an illuminated lens these joinings are often seen in Lapis glaze; they plainly indicate that some uprising of the glaze has occurred. Not infrequently these uprisings fail to level themselves out and can be felt by passing the hand over the surface.

Some other peculiarities of Lapis glaze are also due to the physical condition of the glaze. Its viscous condition, when fused, prevents the bubbles of gas (formed during fusion) from escaping before the glaze cools and congeals. These imprisoned bubbles scatter light and cause colours to take on a softer and quieter hue. Light transmission is further diminished by undissolved glaze material suspended in the glaze in a finely subdivided state. This causes the glaze to be more or less translucent, according to the thickness of the glaze. Where it is thin, as on the rims of bowls or the lip of a vase, it may be nearly transparent; where it is thick, as in hollows, it may appear to be opaque. Hence, on one and the same pot there may be different colour and texture effects from the same glaze.

The shallow dish (Plate 35) is an excellent example of Lapis on a light, slightly harsh, brickish red body. The spirals in the bottom of the dish show extremes of translucence, and an intermediate degree is seen in the plain parts of the design on the rim of the dish. The colour of these plain parts has none of the harshness of the red of the spirals, thus showing the softening effect of translucence on colour. That dish has other Lapis characteristics. Passing a hand over its coloured parts finds upheavals which have not levelled themselves out, and a lens shows them to be charged with small bubbles like a freshly drawn glass of soda water. The mingling of the light and dark green varies from place to place and modifies the artist's design. The mottling of the colour and the effect of the drag down the sides of the dish and the spreading out of the mottled colour at the bottom help to make the piece a fascinating study in colour.

The bulbous vase (left hand of Plate 36) with its sober colour, its flowing lines of mottled blue and its speckling with undissolved pigment, shows the single colour type at its best. The design has outlined itself in the firing by raising every line above the level of the surrounding glaze and at the same time has deprived the glaze immediately outlining it of its colour. A truly remarkable phenomenon.

The uniqueness of Lapis is well seen when contrasted with some other dull or semi-dull glazed ware. A good example of the latter is a variety made by Messrs. Carter, Stabler, and Adams at the

Poole pottery a few years ago. Its glaze is white, opaque, beautifully smooth, and eminently suitable for on-glaze painting. Fine lines and small patterns are painted thereon, and many colours are used. Its appeal to pottery lovers is quite distinct from that of Lapis, for the two are poles apart in style of decoration.

Summarily stated, the differences in style of decoration are:

1. Lapis grounds are tinted, whereas Poole has a near white ground.
2. Lapis designs are indefinitely outlined and have self-mottled and/or speckled flowing colour, whereas Poole designs are sharply outlined and have still and uniform colour.
3. Lapis designs are in the interior of the glaze, whereas Poole designs are on the surface.
4. Lapis uses only a few colours, whereas Poole uses many.

Both wares are fine examples of the potter's craft, and both have deservedly good reputations.

Lapis ware is undoubtedly one of the finest achievements of the potter's craft. It ranks with the translucent white porcelain of the Far East, the coloured alkaline glazes of the Middle East, the iridescent lustre of the Persians, and the copper-red glazes of the Chinese, as an outstanding advance in ceramics. Like them, it exalted the craft and enlarged the area of artistic expression.

It is the fruit of crossing thirty-five years experience of many glazes with a mind scientifically, technically and artistically experienced in the craft. All honour to Joseph Burton for having enriched the world in this signal manner.

CHAPTER 8

Iridescent Lustre Pottery

Behold this cup within whose bowl,
Upon a ground of deepest blue
With yellow lustred stars o'erlaid,
Colours of every tint and hue
Mingle in one harmonious whole.

KERAMOS

It is generally agreed among potters that the production of ware painted with designs in iridescent lustre colours is the most difficult of all ceramic decorative processes. Early this century, Pilkingtons succeeded in reviving it at their Lancastrian pottery works, and continued to make it for the space of thirty years. This revival of a ten-centuries-old art is one of the finest achievements of English potters.

In 1903 William Burton commenced his experiments for iridescent lustre and by 1906 had made sufficient progress to warrant his going ahead. In the meantime much experimental work had been done at the factory on glazes for other purposes, and fortunately, many of them were found to be eminently suitable for the new technique.

The decoration of pottery with iridescent metallic films is one of the most astonishing and beautiful inventions ever made by the potter. These iridescent colours shining and shimmering with the brilliance of mother-of-pearl have furnished us with some of the most beautiful and highly prized of the artistic pottery of bygone centuries. Greatly as the art has been esteemed, both by potters and artists, it has experienced more vicissitudes than fall to the lot of most decorative processes. Indeed for some centuries it was reckoned among the lost arts.

It is supposed to have been invented by Egyptian potters. By the tenth century the Persian potters had acquired the art, and during the next four centuries they frequently produced supremely beautiful pieces. From there the Moors carried the process to Spain, where the famous Hispano-Moresque ware was made. From Spain it passed to Italy where, in the sixteenth century, the ruby-lustred Majolica of Gubbio and the golden-yellow lustres of Deruta were made.

After this period of brilliance the lustre process was apparently lost in Europe for some centuries. It was revived in the second half of the nineteenth century by a number of potters, including Cantegalli in Florence, Massier in France, Zsolnay in Hungary and De Morgan in England. These workers produced admirable copies of mediaeval work as well as interesting departures of their own, but these ventures eventually petered out as did the efforts of many others.

This discontinuance of manufacture is not to be wondered at when it is realised that the process is most uncertain and its results erratic and unpredictable. Few people, even among lovers of pottery, have any real knowledge of what is involved in the making of this beautiful ware. Ceramic literature does not help very much, for it is mostly concerned with the historical aspect of the subject, and with illustrating the works of Persian, Hispano-Moresque, and Italian masters. Apart from two lectures delivered before the Royal Society of Arts, one by William De Morgan, and the other by William Burton, there is little that is informative on the technical aspect of this mysterious and elusive art.

Iridescent lustre is produced by painting on the already fired glaze a compound of silver and/or copper diluted with clay or some other inert material and mixed with some oily or other medium to make the mixture fit for the artist's brush and then firing the ware in a kiln specially constructed for the purpose. At a definite stage in the firing process, described by one fireman as a cherry red heat, the atmosphere in the kiln is changed from an oxidising to a reducing one, by restricting the supply of air to the furnace. This is continued for a time and then the fire is allowed to die out. When cool the kiln is opened and the pieces removed to have the inert diluent washed off.

From this brief account it would seem that the process is a simple one. Actually it is the most sensitive and difficult of all pottery processes. That fact probably explains why so few potters have succeeded in producing iridescent lustre. How difficult the process is can be judged from the experiences of successful producers. A sixteenth-century manuscript describing the process says: 'This art is uncertain in its success, frequently only six pieces being good out of a hundred'. De Morgan said that, at times, his experiences were almost as disheartening, and Pilkingtons suffered many grievous disappointments.

In this difficult art, disappointment and rejoicing walk side by side. Notwithstanding difficulties and vexations, perseverance was rewarded, from time to time, by the appearance of masterpieces. Some of these exceptional pieces were truly magnificent and are worthy to be set beside the finest examples of the past. Long experience in the work taught much, but far from sufficient to prevent the contents of one kiln differing from the contents of the previous kiln, of vase differing from another vase in the same kiln, or even the back of a pot differing from its front.

To what were the masterpieces due? Had we lived in other times we might have explained them in the same way that a director of the Imperial Porcelain Factory at Ching-te-chen explained the many superb pieces that came from the kilns there in the reign of the Emperor K'ang-hsi (1662-1722). Speaking of a director at that time, he said, 'When Ts'ang was director of the porcelain works, the finger of the God was often seen in the midst of the furnace fire, either painting the designs or shielding them from harm, so that the porcelain came out perfect and beautiful'. The potter knows little of what causes results to be erratic, nor does he know how to avoid them with certainty.

What does the potter seek to do? It is generally said that he seeks to produce on the surface of the glaze an exceedingly thin metallic film. This is not strictly true, for such a film of some metals (e.g. platinum) is not iridescent. What the potter seeks to do is to produce a film that will split ordinary daylight into its constituent colours.

There are two kinds of colour; one is produced from material pigments, the other is produced by light. The colours in fabrics are produced from pigments called dyes, and the colour in pictures from pigments called paints. Many garden flowers are coloured by pigments which can be removed from them. The colours from light, such as the blue of the sky, the roseate hues of early dawn and sunset, and of the rainbow after rain, are all purely light-effects.

Ordinary daylight (sometimes called white light) is a mixture of many colours. Normally these different colours remain mixed as white light, but under certain circumstances become separated. This happens when light is bent or refracted, as for instance, by means of a prism or a rain drop, or when reflected from a surface covered with a thin layer of transparent substance. Hence the array of colours seen in the spectrum when light passes through a glass prism, or seen in the rainbow of a shower, or the spray of a fountain, or in a thin layer of oil on the surface of water. It is this assemblage of many colours that is called *iridescence*.

The exceedingly thin films on bird's feathers split white light into its constituent colours, causing the gorgeous iridescent colours of their plumage. The breast feathers of the East African starling are supremely fascinating to the lover of Turquoise colour. It is marvellous that birds, generation after generation, reproduce their colours with such exactitude when a minute change in the thickness of the microscopic film would entirely alter the general appearance.

In seeking to produce iridescent lustre, the potter seeks to produce a film thin enough to reflect light colours. As colour produced by reflected light varies with the incidence of light, the colour changes when either the viewer or the object alter position, thus producing a shimmering sheen of variegated colour, as the birds do. A potter who expects constant results is expecting to equal the birds in constancy.

In the production of iridescent lustre pottery both glaze and method of firing are important factors. The glaze should soften sufficiently to receive and retain metallic vapours, and be adhesive to hold firmly the metallic compounds when once union is made. It is preferable, though not essential, that it should be transparent.

The importance of the firing process cannot be over-estimated. It is fraught with peril. The exceedingly thin metallic film is like a delicate child, very susceptible to influences that play about it. Success and failure hang in the balance and slight changes in the conditions tilt the balance. Exactly what tilts the scales is not known. The secret eludes the potter, yet grips him with irresistible fascination.

With the aid of a little elementary chemistry—the knowledge of what is meant by oxidation and reduction—we can probe more deeply into this mysterious region of the potter's lustring kiln. It is sufficiently accurate for our purpose, though not quite correct, to say that oxidation is the union of oxygen with a metal, and reduction means their separation in such a way that the metal is left.

An excellent example of both oxidation and reduction is afforded by copper. If copper metal is heated in a stream of oxygen the two unite and make a black powder which is copper oxide. If this black oxide is heated in a stream of hydrogen, or a stream of carbon monoxide gas, the oxygen is carried away and the metal left. The term 'reduction' is not confined to the separation of oxygen from metals, it includes other separations. For instance, if the metal silver is placed in a stream of sulphuretted hydrogen, the silver unites with sulphur, forming silver sulphide. If this black powder of silver sulphide is heated in a stream of hydrogen it is deprived of its sulphur and the silver is left behind.

Equipped with this knowledge one can approach the potter and watch what happens as he fires his kiln. With a brightly burning fire he heats the kiln in the usual way to the desired temperature. A brightly burning fire indicates that along with the hot products of combustion there is an excess of oxygen and, therefore, the atmosphere of his kiln is oxidising. When the firing has continued long enough, he piles dry wood on to the fire and restricts the air supply so much that there is insufficient air to burn the fuel completely. Being short of oxygen the atmosphere changes to a reducing one, and reduces the metallic compounds in the painted decoration to the metal state. When this second type of firing has continued long enough, firing ceases, the embers die out and the kiln cools. When it has cooled sufficiently he empties the kiln, somewhat excitedly, for he is anxious to see the results.

Very little is known of what was happening inside the kiln during those hours. The composition of the kiln atmosphere in the second period was very changeable, possibly made up of carbon monoxide, carbon dioxide, nitrogen, water vapour, various hydrocarbons and carbohydrates. The feeding of the furnace being intermittent, the relative proportions of these items were constantly changing. No known method of gas analysis could keep step with those rapid changes.

Besides suitable glaze and firing method there appear to be three other fundamental requisites.

1. SUITABLE METALS. So far, only silver and copper have proved satisfactory. Both of these possess in differing degrees the following

characteristics: (*a*) a relatively low melting temperature; (*b*) volatility or power to form volatile compounds at a low temperature; and (*c*) the ability readily to undergo the chemical changes of oxidation and reduction.

2. CORRECT THICKNESS OF FILM. As differences in the wave lengths of light are exceedingly minute, minutely thin films are requisite to split light into its constituent waves. A soap bubble affords an excellent illustration of this. When first formed a soap bubble film is comparatively thick and transparent. As the film becomes thinner the interference colours (iridescence) formed from light reflected from the film may be seen. If, however, the film lasts long enough to dwindle to a thickness of about 0·0000005 cm. or less, then it will appear black when viewed by reflected light. It is always transparent, and will never be black when viewed by transmitted light. Evidently there is only a narrow range of thickness capable of causing iridescence.

3. AN OXIDISED FILM. It is well known that metals which do not tarnish on exposure to air do not lend themselves to iridescence. That fact explains why, for instance, platinum does not give iridescence. But the corollary—that oxygen may be necessary for the production of iridescence—has apparently been overlooked. Indeed it is said that oxygen must be excluded from the kiln during the last stage of firing, and that idea dominates the practice of lustre firing. Metallurgy, however, seems to indicate that the idea may be erroneous. If hard steel with a polished surface is gradually heated in air, it assumes a colour which changes as the temperature rises, eventually reaching purple, violet and blue. When tempering steel the blacksmith heats it to a higher temperature than he needs and then allows it to cool. The colour gradually changes and when it arrives at the particular hue he needs he quenches it in water. Scientific investigation has shown that the colour is due to a thin film of oxidised metal, the particular hue assumed depending on the thickness of the film, the temperature, and the rate of cooling.

If those considerations hold good for ceramic lustre, the thin reduced metal film formed on the glaze surface during firing needs reoxidising. But how, seeing that the last stage of the firing is done in a reducing atmosphere?

I venture to suggest that the explanation is found in what happens after the firing has ceased. Chemical action inside the kiln does not cease when the embers in the furnace box die out. The walls of the firing chamber being made of porous fireclay blocks allow the heavier and cooler air outside to percolate into the interior of the kiln. This cooler air displaces the hot reducing gases that are therein. In consequence, the atmosphere inside the kiln gradually becomes oxidising, weakly at first, but intensifying as the proportion of fresh air increases. At the same time there is a gradual fall in temperature. As the oxidation of metals such as copper and silver is slower at low temperatures and weaker if the action is of short duration, it is conceivable that at some period during the cooling the conditions are favourable to the right amount of reoxidation necessary for an iridescent film. That may be the explanation of this baffling problem.

Biographical

By now the reader is aware of the tremendous impression that was created by the phenomenal advent of Royal Lancastrian Pottery when it suddenly appeared in 1904. The first section of this book tells the story of the birth and development of the ware but says little about the great efforts that were needed to raise it to the high level of excellence it eventually attained.

The second section partly fills in the omission by bringing to the reader's notice evidences of bustling activities behind the scenes. It provides a picture of keen minds wrestling with problems new and old and of others probing the unknown in search of what lies there involving the testing of ideas and, on occasion, ignoring custom and convention.

This third section which we are now entering will provide biographical sketches of the persons who originated the ware and gave it its exceptional characteristics and thereby left their impress upon it. Naturally, the section begins with the founder of the ware, William Burton.

CHAPTER 9

The Burton Family

Wᴵᴸᴸᴵᴬᴹ ʙᵁᴿᵀᴼᴺ was born on the 19th March 1863, and his brother Joseph on the 16th November 1868, both of them at Droylsden Road, Newton Heath, Manchester, where their father David Burton had a small grocer's shop. David was born at Crawshawbooth, a village in the Rossendale area of Lancashire. Being of Quaker stock he used to attend the Meeting House there. Besides William and Joseph there were three other children in the family.

Later, after settling in Manchester, David Burton associated himself with the Quakers at their Meeting House in Mount Street, Manchester. He and John Bright often walked together to the Meeting on Sundays, Joseph walking behind them. David and his wife, though simple folk, were Elders in the Society and so were amongst those who sat in the 'Minister's Gallery' at the head of the large gathering in the Meeting House on Sunday mornings. He was not eloquent of speech, nor profound in thought, yet was listened to most attentively; his words, sensible and sometimes quaint, were winged with transparent sincerity and deep humility. He was of good repute and respected in a community which was mainly cultured and well educated.

He is remembered for his generous nature, his kindliness, and his readiness to help. Into his small grocer's shop came the needy, the troubled, and the distressed, seeking help and advice. The neighbours consulted him on all sorts of affairs. Without any formal legal knowledge he gave sound advice as he served in the shop, and many a quarrel was settled or perplexity solved without recourse to solicitors.

He was more of a saint than a business man. Some even went so far as to speak of him as Saint David. In a monetary sense, he died a poor man, but his passing on was that of one rich in the affections of the people. His sudden unexpected death was widely mourned; by a natural response and without any publicity, people lined both sides of the road for several hundred yards as the short plain funeral procession passed by.

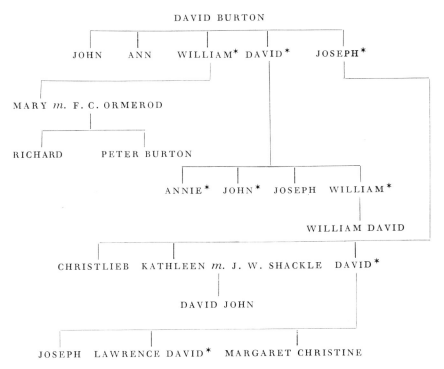

* *Employed at the Lancastrian Pottery*

WILLIAM BURTON, M.A.

William Burton, together with his brothers David and Joseph, began his education at a Methodist day school associated with Culcheth Methodist Chapel, near where they lived, of which the headmaster was an Irishman named Lakin. William Burton became a pupil teacher there and, later, an assistant schoolmaster. He left to be assistant master in Chemistry and Physics under the Manchester School Board, when the Central Higher Grade School was opened in 1884. In his early days he learned all his Science in the evening schools of the Manchester School Board and in evening classes at Owens College. In 1885, he gained the premier national scholarship of the year in science and went to the Royal School of Mines, where he worked in Professor Thorpe's chemical laboratory. Here he made the acquaintance of H. G. Wells and the two became fast friends. Eager to be in a settled job after his own heart and equally eager to settle down as a married man, he threw up his college career in its last year and went to the Potteries to be chemist at Messrs. Josiah Wedgwood & Sons' pottery. In his hurry he sacrificed the opportunity of acquiring a degree by examination.

He was at Wedgwood's from 1887 until 1892, when he removed to Clifton Junction. During these five years in the Potteries, he was frequently advocating the application of science to pottery making. He taught classes in technical pottery at the Wedgwood Institute in Burslem and in the Science Schools in Hanley. He delivered several lectures on the subject in the district. His removal to Clifton did not diminish his efforts in this direction. He was gifted with fluent speech, clear enunciation, lucidity of thought and apt expression. These gifts allied to a wide and ever increasing knowledge of the history, craft, art, and science of pottery caused him to be in great demand as a lecturer. He gave several lectures before the Royal Society of Arts, also at South Kensington Museum at the request of the Board of Education. In the Manchester area, too, he often lectured. On occasions he would take with him E. T. Radford, the famous thrower, with a potter's wheel to demonstrate the craft of pottery-making.

He was a man with vision, ability, ideas and abounding energy. The starting of a large new works among people unaccustomed to

25. David Burton senr. (1825-1888), aged 50.

By courtesy of Mrs. J. W. Shackle

26. William Burton, M.A. (1863-1941) in 1908, aged 45.

27. Joseph Burton (1868-1934), in 1911 aged 42.

Loaned by the author

28

Yours sincerely
Gordon M. Forsyth

the industry with its multitude of technical, commercial, industrial and administrative problems, is enough to tax to the full the energy of any ordinary man. William Burton coped with these responsibilities and undertook others of importance. He became examiner in Pottery and Porcelain for the City and Guilds of London Institute and entirely remodelled its syllabus. When the lead-poisoning agitation was afoot he was one of the chief exponents of the manufacturers' point of view, and he served as a member of the Departmental Committee to advise the Board of Trade on the matter. He also wrote a book on the subject for the Pottery Manufacturers' Association. He was, for many years the Chairman of the Association, which, in his case meant taking a very active part in its affairs. In addition, he catalogued many private and public collections. Over a wide span of years he lived a strenuous life crowded with unceasing labours.

He had a remarkable flair for selecting the right people. All those key-workers who came with him at the beginning were, I believe, without exception, successes. Most of them remained to the end of their working lives. Though he possessed that flair he did not disdain the advice of others when selecting people for important positions. His selective instinct served him well as he gathered round him artists whose individuality, aesthetic sense, creative ability and expertness afterwards conferred such great distinction on the ware.

His mental capabilities were exceptional. The rapid advance he made in his student days is an indication of his facility for acquiring knowledge. His receptive mind quickly assimilated and set in order the varied and unco-ordinated ideas that poured into it. I went occasionally to his house in the evenings to take down as he dictated the substance of his books. So effortlessly did the words come from his lips that it seemed as if his voice was the course along which flowed a copious clear stream.

His versatility was extraordinary. He was a capable teacher, lecturer, advocate, author, translator, scientist, artist, historian, potter, director, and especially a leader and inspirer of others. Showmanship, too, was in his repertoire; how otherwise could he have so successfully organised and arranged a display of his wares at Graves Gallery, and that most impressive display at the Franco-British exhibition? Both of these succeeded in obtaining great publicity. He made contact with life at many points. His circle of acquaintances was wide and included many close friends. He consorted with artists and other cultured people. He was a welcome guest in many places. Potters requited his frank openness with their confidences. 'The Hollies', where he dwelt with wife and daughter was a magnet that drew people from far and near. Such a full life added ideas, knowledge and inspiration. All was grist that came to his mill. The central purpose of his life was Lancastrian Pottery and everything must make its contribution to that.

In his student days, both he and H. G. Wells were zealous socialists and proclaimed it by wearing red ties. They went to meetings of the Fabian Society and occasionally read papers and had debates and discussions among the students. Wells describes him thus: 'Old Burton, Ruskinised, biblical as became a man from John Bright's Manchester, and very eloquent and copious'. His later political leanings are perhaps indicated by the fact that Miss Sylvia Pankhurst and other suffragettes were entertained at his home at Clifton Junction.

Soon after he went to Wedgwood's he married Eliza Nicholls, youngest of the eleven children of John Nicholls (a farmer) and Eliza Nicholls, of Bury Hall, Wolverley, Worcestershire. They lived in a little house at Basford not far from the Wedgwood pot bank at Etruria. When H. G. Wells had stayed at their home for several weeks, he told an acquaintance that he found their books and their talk and the strange landscape with its blazing iron foundries, its canals, its clay whitened pot banks and the marvellous effects of its dust and smoke on the atmosphere at sunset very stimulating.

When the Burtons removed to Clifton they lived for a time in one of a row of small houses until 'The Hollies' was ready for them. They had one daughter, Mary, who helped her father in many ways, particularly in the cataloguing of the famous Salting collection of pottery in the Victoria and Albert Museum.

Like his father before him William Burton had a generous disposition and he gave help unstintingly to many people. Two whose names were later adorned with the coveted letters R.A. owe their advancement in some measure to him. One was Charles E. Cundall, whom he brought from Ackworth school to paint pots under the tutorship of Gordon M. Forsyth. The other was Francis Dodd. Another artist whom he helped was Bertram Nicholls, son of Alderman William Nicholls of Manchester, and a nephew of Mrs. Burton, who was President of the Academy of Fine Arts for ten years, and also President of the Royal Society of British Artists.

In keeping with this spirit of helpfulness William Burton was one of the founder members of the Northern Art Workers' Guild to encourage and develop art among craft workers. He was its president in 1908. Among his public activities was membership of a committee appointed by the Board of Education for the re-arrangement of the Victoria and Albert Museum. He was a member of the Manchester Literary and Philosophical Society and a valued contributor to the *Manchester Guardian*.

Many names adorn ceramics in this country. No one embraced it so completely as did William Burton. Natural aptitude, education and training, intense interest, ever widening knowledge and experience—all enabled him to appreciate its every aspect. Its history, science, art, technology and craftsmanship; its fascination, loveliness and utility, were all within his province. In every one, he was regarded as an expert; he touched all these sides. His touch, unlike that of Midas, was enriching and fructifying. It is a great satisfaction to recall that he was not without honour in his own country. Twice, the Royal Society of Arts presented him with its

91

silver medal. The Manchester University showed its appreciation of his work by conferring on him in 1908 the honorary degree of Master of Arts. When Chairman of the Pottery Manufacturers' Association his fellow-members invited him to accept nomination as candidate for Parliament for the Stoke-on-Trent division. The sitting member (Col. John Ward, M.P.) assured him that he would stand aside, as nothing would induce him to oppose one who had done so much for the pottery industry. William Burton declined nomination. He was also offered but declined a knighthood.

The obituary notice which appeared in the *Pottery Gazette* summarised the opinion held of him by the industry. It reads, 'William Burton, who has rendered long and eminent service to pottery, was one of the industry's outstanding personalities of modern times, for, in addition to being a trained chemist and a fundamentally trained potter, who never disdained the legitimate use of machinery in modern production he was also aesthetically minded, and coupled with an immense knowledge of ceramic history such as is seldom evidenced, he was possessed of an unerring instinct for beauty. He had a rare understanding of art in industry, and although he was notable not so much as an executant in the design of pottery, he was a great inspirer of other men's best work. He possessed the unusual gift of understanding artists thoroughly and of knowing how to call forth their best efforts. His mental make-up was acknowledged to be exceptional, if not phenomenal, and he was so well informed in all branches of potting as to be regarded in the nature of an all-round authority, for he could just as easily discuss complex problems of manufacture or organisation as he could adjudicate upon the finer points of craftsmanship or art. He was truly a great personality. He was exceptionally generous hearted, and, apart from his natural outstanding ability, this was perhaps his greatest quality. In the words of another writer—he never refused kindly advice and practical help to any in trouble, and the many distinguished visitors who visited Clifton Junction—writers, artists and connoisseurs in ceramics—were all entertained in a princely manner and invariably carried away a choice example of the potter's art'.

It is written of the illustrious chemist, Hofmann, that he had a marvellous power of stimulating his students and imparting to them his enthusiasm. And it is said of James Morton, who can be regarded as the principal founder of the 'Vat' dyestuffs industry in Britain, that he had the power of attracting disciples who remained not merely his fellow-workers but one with himself in a passionate determination to carry their mission to success. William Burton belongs to that same high rank. Similar things can be said of him for, in all who came under his spell, he kindled and fed the flames of interest, enthusiasm, and desire to excel. This strange power emanated from him effortlessly; he was a genius in whom artist and scientist were combined in an effusive and dominating personality.

What a mighty work he wrought in such a short time! 1893 to 1903 were ten years of preparation; 1903 to 1915 were twelve years of achievement. How crowded a life he lived! How deep an impression he carved! His strenuous life was lived at high pressure. To live at that rate until he had passed fifty years of age was a great achievement, but it could not last, for he was wearing himself out. Strenuousness without intermission exacted her penalty, his health failed, and the 'art of the potter' lost its *Maestro*.

On his retirement in August 1915, he was presented with an illuminated address bound in book form, accompanied with a silver bowl, chased and enamelled, with lapis-lazuli jewels inset. The address reads:

Dear Mr. William Burton. We, the underwritten, desire to convey to you, on your retirement from the management of Pilkington's Tile and Pottery Company, Limited, our appreciation of your many thoughtful acts and kindnesses to all who came under your direction, and especially so to those who have at any time been in trouble. You have always been in the forefront in all matters concerning the health of the workers, and the pioneer of many reforms in the present-day British ceramic art and manufacture. We recall to mind your appointment and work on the Government Commission and Committees for the investigation of the working conditions in the tile and pottery industry generally; your chairmanship of the Tile Manufacturers' Association and Potters' Insurance Committees. We know that thereby you have been able to lead the way to improved conditions of pottery labour in its many branches, and that you have also interested a wider public by your lectures and literary contributions on the history and manufacture of pottery and porcelain, gaining in addition the appreciation and honour of one of our most progressive universities. It is our earnest hope that good health will return to you, and that the ceramic industry will be further benefited by your influence. Simply and sincerely we have expressed what we feel, and are sure you will accept this book and cup along with our heartfelt remembrances. Yours faithfully (the names of the employees following).

An account of the presentation appeared in the *Manchester Guardian* on 13th August 1915. In the same issue is the following: 'It is not the workpeople of the remarkable pottery works of which William Burton has, for a quarter of a century been manager who alone will regret his retirement or the cause of it. Manchester perhaps has not even yet fully realised that on its borders and within a few minutes run by train, some of the finest pottery in Europe is produced and it may well be that the output of the works at Clifton Junction is better known to the experts of Berlin and Paris than it is to all but a comparatively few nearer home. Yet we cannot claim so many artistic glories that we should think lightly of this one. Of this fine development Mr. Burton is the inspirer and the artistic and scientific head. For in the making of the best pottery there is, needless to say, as much of science—largely chemical science—as of art, and in both Mr. Burton excelled. His knowledge of the whole history and development of his craft is immense and its rich fruit is to be found in many beautiful pages of the latest edition of the *Encyclopaedia Britannica*. He has another title to fame. Like every true craftsman he was one with his men. There was never any doubt as to who was master in his establishment, but he understood and cared for those with and by whom he worked as one of themselves, and they all knew it and responded to it. The little tribute from them which we record today is but the symbol of what they owe and feel.'

William Burton towered head and shoulders above all others in the early years of Royal Lancastrian Pottery's development. He conceived the idea, gave it form, nursed it through infancy, supplied the initial knowledge, fed it continually, and surmounted its obstacles. He it was who selected the key-workers, encouraged and stimulated them, consulted experts, enlisted the help of advisers, and created comradeship in the adventure. He infused them with faith in its ultimate triumph. He saw to it that its fame should be noised abroad, using press and platform skilfully for the purpose. Throughout it all his brother Joseph was at his side slowly and surely gaining knowledge and experience. They pooled their knowledge and ideas. They spent much time together wrestling with the problems that confronted them. Most likely it was after consulting together that they individually brought to me ideas for experiments. William suggested to me all the ideas for flambé glaze trials, and gave me suggestions for zinc crystalline glazes. Joseph told me how to make the experiments for the eggshell glaze which has since been used for half a century. He also suggested to me how to make leadless glazes and lead frits that were non-toxic. The two collaborated so closely that none can say of what was achieved in the years they were together, 'This was William's and that was Joseph's'. I, who was their right-hand man on the chemical side right from the beginning, cannot apportion the credit, and indeed it cannot be done. In the inner circle of those well acquainted with these matters Lancastrian ware was regarded as a joint product.

This sketch of William Burton would be incomplete did it not contain something about the hospitality at 'The Hollies', the house on the hillside looking southward down the Irwell Valley.

Mrs. Burton was a charming hostess, intensely interested in the work of her many and varied guests, a good talker and a good listener. The house was not equipped with a telephone, the shops were far away and in those days refrigerators were unknown, yet she proved equal to numerous unexpected demands. She was infinitely resourceful in providing meals for groups of people at an hour's notice. Her husband thought nothing of sending a boy from the works to say that he was bringing four or six guests in to lunch, and would a meal be ready for them at one o'clock.

Among those who were privileged to enjoy the delightful hospitality and good fellowship of this home were many leading Continental potters, for he enjoyed a high European reputation. These included M. Auscher, head of the State Porcelain Works at Sèvres, who came with his wife and son; the director of the Royal Copenhagen factory, and the director of the Delft Pottery; all these were entertained for some days. Every Sunday evening, a large circle of Manchester artists came to supper. The well-known designers Lewis F. Day and Walter Crane frequently stayed for a few days as did other distinguished visitors like Sir Hercules Read of the British Museum and Sir Arthur Whitelegge, Chief of the Factory Department at the Home Office.

One afternoon two strange figures arrived; one very dark with a dark beard, and dressed in black; the other fair and dressed in brilliant colours. They were Lytton Strachey and Henry Lamb, the former looking exactly like the portrait of him painted by Lamb.

Many members of the staff of the Manchester University came. Among them were close friends of Mr. Burton—viz. Sir Alfred Hopkinson (the Vice-Chancellor), Sir Grafton Elliot Smith and Professors Tout and Dixon. He was drawn to Dixon as a fellow chemist, and to Tout and Elliot Smith by a common interest in history. On one visit there was a long discussion between Elliot Smith and him as to whether the turquoise glazed statuettes found in Egyptian tombs were in fact pottery or glazed carved sandstone. These two distinguished men and their families remained firm

friends and neighbours until their deaths shortly before the outbreak of World War II.

Others who came included Sir Arthur Schuster, Sir Ernest
Rutherford (later Lord Rutherford, o.m.) and Professor Horace
Lamb.

I trust it will not be considered inappropriate if I attempt some
appreciation of William Burton's place in the hierarchy of English
potters. Very few are alive today who worked with him at Clifton
Junction, and of these I am the only one who worked with him on
the chemical and technical side of the industry.

Josiah Wedgwood was the greatest European potter of the
eighteenth century. Alexander Brongniart, the director of the
Royal Porcelain factory at Sèvres was the outstanding potter of the
nineteenth century. William Burton wrote of the former: 'His influence was so powerful, and his personality so dominant that all
the other English potters worked on the principles he had laid
down and thus a fresh impulse and a new direction was given to
the pottery of England and of the civilised world. It may be truly
said that the whole subsequent course of pottery manufacture has
been influenced by his individuality, skill, and taste'. Of Brongniart
he wrote: 'He it was who gathered together a band of experiment-
ers, practical potters, modellers, and painters of the period, and co-
ordinated their separate industries to one end'.

Much of the language William Burton used concerning his two
famous predecessors can be fittingly applied to himself. His mighty
work was wrought in the early years of the present century, and so
powerfully has he influenced the development of the art and technique of pottery, that it is not inaccurate to describe him as the
pre-eminent potter of the twentieth century, so far.

True it is that in particular branches of the industry he was
excelled by others. In the exceedingly difficult work of reproducing
the alkaline glazed pottery of the Persians William de Morgan
possibly succeeded better than did William Burton. Bernard Moore

97

was a more experienced and more successful pottery experimental-
ist, and also had a fuller and more intimate knowledge of the craft's
peculiarities, and in after years Joseph Burton had a more thorough
understanding and appreciation of glaze quality than had his more
famous brother. It was William's many-sided activities that raised
him to a position of commanding superiority.

Our two distinguished English potters had many things in
common. Both were public-spirited men and rendered valuable
service to their fellow potters in matters pertaining to the whole
of the industry. Their intimate knowledge of all branches of the
industry combined with their exceptional gifts eminently fitted
them to lead the industry in defence against attacks on their
liberties. In Wedgwood's time it was against the granting of a
monopoly to a competitor, and in William Burton's time it was
against a stranglehold on their use of lead compounds in glazes.

William Burton's rise to eminence in the esteem of his fellow
potters was rapid. Twelve years after entering the industry as a
raw recruit he was welcomed by them as a leader jointly with
Bernard Moore. This rapid rise came not through accident or
chance or favour, but naturally, through their quick recognition
of his outstanding abilities. He merited the position and requited
their trust by thorough, painstaking, and assiduous labours in their
causes, particularly so through the lead poisoning agitation which
vexed the industry for many years. He afterwards said that the
time he had devoted to that difficult problem was equal to two
years of his life, which is a big slice to give to what was largely
disinterested service.

Both men were alike in being leaders in the application of science
to the pottery industry. In Wedgwood's day the science of chemistry was passing through a long infancy. It was not much more than
a medley of unrelated facts and observations and possessed little
knowledge of the underlying laws governing chemical activity. The
idea of an atomic constitution of matter, which is the foundation

upon which modern chemistry is built, was then unknown unless as a speculation.

Wedgwood's questing spirit compelled him to seek increased knowledge by experiments. The voluminous note books he has left behind testify to the extent and thoroughness of his efforts, and emphasise his insatiable thirst for new knowledge. Out of it came forth two triumphant achievements; one, the well-known Jasper stoneware, which has added so much to the glories of decorative pottery, and the other, the invention of his famous pyrometer.

This instrument was invented by him in 1783. It is the first instrument ever made for the scientific measuring of the effect produced by heat at high temperatures. Truly, a noteworthy achievement. The accompanying drawing is of one kindly loaned by Messrs. Josiah Wedgwood & Sons for the purpose of this book.

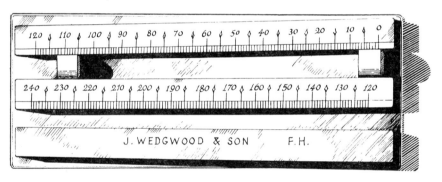

Wedgwood's pyrometer, invented 1783.

The instrument consists of a brass plate to which are affixed two other pieces of brass 0·5 inch apart at one end and 0·3 inch apart at the other end, thus forming a gradually narrowing space. This space he divided into 'degrees' by marks upon the brass. Down the narrowing space were slid little rolls of clay which had first been baked at a temperature sufficient to expel the combined water in the clay. They were then placed in the oven and fired with the ware. As the firing progressed they contracted more and more, and from time to time one was taken out and after having cooled was again slid down the instrument. The difference in measurement before and after firing was a measure of the contraction that had taken place, and this enabled the fireman to judge the progress that had been made in firing the ware. The instrument thus measured the effect of heat on clay. It is not used now, for Seger cones and Holdcroft's thermoscopes show the same effect by an alteration in shape which can be seen whilst the firing is in progress.

I have inserted this description of Wedgwood's pyrometer because there is no mention of it in many scientific text-books on pyrometry. For a century after its discovery nothing was discovered to supersede it; indeed nothing yet has superseded the principle on which it is based. Science students grow up unaware of this beacon light in the measuring of the effect of heat on clay at high temperatures. Its discovery in the dim scientific light of the eighteenth century was a great achievement and placed Wedgwood among the pioneers of science.

No written records of William Burton's individual work have been preserved. No scientific instrument is labelled with his name. Nevertheless, he was a great scientist. Upon a foundation of science he built a great name and a great industry. He stimulated his staff to scientific methods and research, and he imbued his fellow potters with a sense of their value.* The great advance in the application of science to the pottery industry is largely the product of his insistent labours to that end.

Both men recognised that art could render great service in the enrichment of pottery. Wedgwood's Jasper ware owes much of its fame to the figures modelled by that master sculptor, John Flaxman, and his associates. Lancastrian Pottery likewise owes much of its reputation to that group of artists who, under the inspiring influence of its chief designer, Gordon M. Forsyth, and the sugges-

* See the *Staffordshire Sentinel*, 12th January 1904.

tions of eminent designers like Walter Crane, produced master-pieces of painted lustre pottery. William Burton's acquaintance with the works of ancient art in the potters' craft and his ability to appreciate the finer qualities of pottery art generally, made him welcome in art circles and helped to fit him for directing the artistic side of Lancastrian Pottery, which he did throughout his association with it.

Both men understood clays and glazes and the various processes in pottery manufacture according to the knowledge of their times. Both continually explored fresh avenues of the potters' art and craft. Both tried out the value of new materials as they were discovered, and new methods as they learned of them and by their aid unfolded new riches. Both men enjoyed European reputations as potters. William Burton knew personally many of the porcelain makers in Europe and visited very many porcelain factories as a welcome guest.

Besides all these similarities there were, of course, differences. Josiah Wedgwood was a practical potter accustomed to the actual making of pots by hand, and was renowned for his skill as a thrower. William Burton was not a worker in clay; he was a great worker with the pen, writing in a smoothly flowing style which is easy to read and assimilate. His books are highly informative without being cumbered with too much detail. They rank high in ceramic literature.

In the distant future when these two famous potters are seen in truer perspective; when due allowance can be made for the difference in their opportunities and in their educational advantages, it may be possible to get a just appraisement of their respective contributions to the advancement of pottery. It is conceivable that in that day William Burton may be regarded as being not much, if any, behind Josiah Wedgwood. This prediction will surprise many and perhaps stimulate some to seek the truth for themselves. The comparison just made appears to justify it.

LIST OF BOOKS WRITTEN BY
MR. WILLIAM BURTON, M.A., F.C.S.

1899   'The Use of Lead Compounds in Pottery'

1902   'A History and Description of English Porcelain'

1904   'A History and Description of English Earthenware and
        Stoneware'

1906   'Porcelain. A Sketch of its Nature, Art and Manufacture'

1909   'Marks on Pottery and Porcelain' (in conjunction with
        R. L. Hobson)

1921   'A General History of Porcelain'

1922   'Josiah Wedgwood and His Pottery'

1910   Parts of the Article on Ceramics in the Eleventh Edition of
        the *Encyclopaedia Britannica*

1893 ⎫ Articles on Pottery and Porcelain in Two Editions of
1913 ⎭ Thorpe's *Dictionary of Applied Chemistry*

1905   An English Translation of E. S. Auscher's *History and
        Description of French Porcelain*

LIST OF LECTURES BEFORE THE
ROYAL SOCIETY OF ARTS
AND PUBLISHED BY THEM

1896   'The Palette of the Potter'

1897   A series of four lectures on 'Material and Design in Pottery'

1901   'Recent Advances in Pottery Decoration'

1904   'Crystalline Glazes and Their Application to the Decoration
        of Pottery'

1907   'Lustre Pottery'

1908   'The Hygiene of the Pottery Trade'

JOSEPH BURTON

After attending the Culcheth Methodist day-school Joseph Burton
went to the well-known Quaker school at Ackworth. Later, he
attended classes in Manchester and obtained an Exhibition to the

Royal College of Science at Dublin, where science was his principal subject.

Like his more famous brother, he was a scientist—particularly in the branches of chemistry, physics, and mineralogy, but he was much more a practical than a theoretical scientist. He was, too, a pioneer in the application of Science to Industry and right from his early days at the pottery he insisted, both by precept and example, on its application. He had imbibed—and it had become part of his being—the scientist's golden rule 'observe, reflect, experiment'. Over and over again did he emphasise the importance of close observation. I fancy that he had been deeply impressed with the story of the discovery of argon and the other rare gases of the atmosphere. That discovery, as chemists well know, resulted from it having been observed that the density of nitrogen obtained from the atmosphere was always slightly greater than that of nitrogen prepared from nitrogen compounds. Investigation revealed that atmospheric nitrogen contained a small quantity of a gas heavier than nitrogen (argon); hence the difference in density, and hence the importance of keen observation. To impress more firmly this idea in my mind he took me to a meeting of the Manchester Literary and Philosophical Society to hear Professor Ramsay lecture on the rare gases of the atmosphere. When he saw that I was making use of the 'Periodicity of the Elements' in my glaze experiments he loaned me the English translation of Mendeléeff's classic work on the subject.

It may be that his influence on me in this way, and particularly his insistence on the importance of small differences, is responsible for two of Lancastrian Pottery's most famous glazes. The strikingly beautiful orange-vermilion glaze, and the frit that was the base which yielded those novel glaze effects that have been described earlier, were both the outcome of noticing unusual phenomena.

He pursued this subject when addressing the English Ceramic Society on his retirement from its presidency in 1916. 'Scientific method,' he said, 'means observation, reflection, experiment, not excluding imagination'. He continued: 'To the trained mind no fact or phenomenon stands alone and isolated, but is always seen in relationship to other facts, the mind working intuitively in this direction by habit and so, often enough, things which seem of no importance whatever to the ordinary observer are really significant to the trained man, who immediately recognises their place in the scheme of things, where they may form an important link in the chain of causes and effects and throw light upon a difficult problem. Nothing that happens in the course of manufacture is insignificant, no detail is negligible and scientific method can be profitably applied in every department and to every process'.

The above is taken from Volume 15 of the Society's *Transactions*, and so is the following account of some experiments he made.

'When I first commenced to experiment in coloured glazes some 25 years ago, it occurred to me that I might try the effect of precipitated chromate of iron in an ordinary unstained majolica glaze. I expected that, in suitable proportions, I should get a canary yellow glaze, but I had no more definite knowledge than that at hand. I made a series of five stained glazes increasing the amount by regular stages, until, in the last of the series, the proportion of stain was, in my judgment, excessive. When the results came out of the kiln I found that the second trial of the series gave me a useful canary yellow glaze, and that the last trial had produced a glaze in which a few small crystals were noticeable. I at once made this last trial the starting point for another series of experiments, which resulted in the production of a certain type of crystalline glaze which we have since used on our ware.' This was the 'Sunstone' glaze referred to in Chapter 2.

His scientific activities at the works were not confined to chemistry. He early introduced the electro-magnet into the slip house to eliminate metallic iron which would cause spots and stains on

the ware. He was quick to employ the thermo-couple electric pyrometer for measuring the temperature of biscuit ovens. These aids
came from outside; indeed he welcomed ideas wherever they came
from, but he did not wait for the outsider, as his own mind was so
fertile. He tried out many ideas in the construction of ovens and
kilns; he was frequently seeking for improvements in the arrangement of flues in biscuit ovens. It was no uncommon thing for him
when rebuilding an oven to try out a new layout of flues for the
more even distribution of the heat. I remember an early recupera-
tive kiln built for the more economical use of coal which proved
unsuccessful because the rise in temperature was too fast to be controlled. I also remember him showing me working drawings of a
tunnel oven, shortly before I left, which was before any such ovens
had been erected in this country.

He was an *artist* in much the same way as his brother; that is,
he was not an executant, but an inspirer of other men. In the later
period of Royal Lancastrian pottery manufacture he was responsible for what might be called the artistic policy of the firm. Will
Mycock, one of the artists who worked with him for forty years,
said of him, 'His love and appreciation of Chinese art of the Sung
and Ming periods caused him to insist upon getting from the
artists designs and treatments which were quiet and restrained. To
my mind his taste and judgment in these matters were invaluable'.
In consequence, a gradual change came over the ware. Whereas
in Forsyth's time there was an element of boldness, in later times
this was absent. It suited Joseph's taste to have the brilliant colour
effects of the Orange-Vermilion glaze diminished by simple brushwork patterns of a suitable dark brown colour and when he produced the Lapis style of decoration with soft colours in tinted
grounds of velvety glaze he found it an exquisite way of expressing
one conception of quality.

He was a *great potter*—one of the greatest in the somewhat
limited sphere in which his activities were spent. His lecture on

'Quality in Pottery' (see Trans. of the English Ceramic Society, Vol. XXIX) is probably the best interpretation ever written on the subject. It reveals a sure grasp of essentials, a true appreciation of characteristics, a rare sensitiveness to minute differences combined with ability to judge their values, and a full knowledge of factors telling for or against quality. He was justly regarded as an expert in these matters.

Along with this sensitiveness to and appreciation of glaze-quality he possessed a remarkable gift or *flair* for sensing the possibilities in new glazes. A striking example of this is his transformation of the ultramarine blue. As originally produced this colour was too vivid to be of real service. As it was a 'pure' colour, i.e., no other blue put alongside it ever dulled it, it could withstand admixture of small amounts of other colour without suffering depreciation. He succeeded in modifying it to a delectable shade, known by various names, but principally as 'Kingfisher' blue, which became very popular and of which thousands of pieces were sold. In a similar way, he made modifications of the brilliant orange-vermilion glaze.

His invention of *Lapis Ware*, which is described in Chapter 7, is another striking example of sensitivity to glaze quality combined with perception of possibilities. That fine ware is the outcome of insight into the peculiar characteristics of the glaze used in its production. Some consider it to be the greatest of the Lancastrian potters' achievements; it certainly must be accorded a very high place in the craft of the potter.

He was also a *great industrialist*. In surveying what is written in this book Joseph Burton seems to be overshadowed by his brother. To put this matter in proper proportion would require mention of many things that do not quite fit a work describing a particular kind of pottery ware. It should be borne in mind that its manufacture was a side-line at a large tile-making works, which was continually growing in size and importance in the industry.

The responsibility of management was his. The planning and supervising of structural developments were his. Technological progress
occupied much of his time. All matters pertaining to the firing process were his concern. These great responsibilities continually calling for attention monopolised most of his time in the years when
his brother was at the helm. He succeeded his brother as general
manager and held the position until his death in 1934.

The collaboration of the two brothers in the development of
Lancastrian Pottery has already been mentioned. All that now
needs to be said is that running together in double harness they
raised the venture to heights of glory. That was its Golden Age. In
that era the masterpieces were produced. Later, when decline
became evident, Joseph, by his introduction of Lapis decoration,
added new glory to the scene, but it was autumn's glow following
summer's radiant splendour.

The two brothers were as alike as two peas in some respects, and
as unlike as chalk and cheese in others. Physically and mentally
William roamed, but Joseph stayed put. William's imagination
flamed with the fiery reds of Chinese flambé glazes, reflected the
brilliant colours of Persian pottery and was intrigued with the
radiating crystals of continental potters. Joseph's quieter mood
found joy in the dulcet tones of the glazes of the Sung dynasty. In
other interests than pottery the difference was wide indeed.

Joseph married Amy Christlieb Connolly, the daughter of a
Protestant clergyman of Foynes, Co. Limerick, Ireland. Three
children were born to them; two daughters and a son. Though he
was acquainted with many cultured people and he himself a man
of wide general culture with a good knowledge of painting and
music, his home was not the scene of animated gatherings as was
that of his brother.

He formed few close friendships but they were lasting ones. His
closest friend was Dr. John James Butterworth, who, for nearly
thirty years, was Medical Officer of Health and School Medical

Officer of the Lancashire County Council. They became acquainted in 1904 and their friendship continued till Joseph's death parted them in 1934. The common ground on which they first met was interest in pottery. An invitation to visit the works was given on the first night they met. The two soon became firm friends and companions, regularly meeting at each other's houses, going long walks together, and together watching cricket at Old Trafford, soccer on the grounds of the two Manchester clubs and occasionally rugby at Swinton. With the passage of time, their association ripened into the intimate friendship of kindred spirits, and thus was a rich experience for both of them.

CHAPTER 10

The Artists

G. M. Forsyth – W. S. Mycock – R. Joyce – C. E. Cundall
G. M. Rodgers

As THE contributions of William and Joseph Burton to the art side of the ware are described in the preceding chapter, they are not included in this chapter.

GORDON MITCHELL FORSYTH, A.R.C.A., R.I., F.R.S.A.
Gordon Forsyth was born in Fraserburgh, Aberdeenshire, and educated at Robert Gordon's College, Aberdeen, and Gray's School of Art. From the school he won a Royal Exhibition to the Royal College of Art, London. In his second year there, he won the college travelling scholarship for design, and as a result studied art in Italy. In 1906 he was put in charge of the artists at Pilkingtons' pottery at Clifton Junction. During the first world war he served the Royal Air Force as a designer of mechanical targets, 1916-1919. He returned to Pilkingtons for a short time. In 1920 he was appointed Superintendent of Art Instruction in Stoke-on-Trent where he remained until he reached retiring age in 1945. He was also Art Advisor to the British Pottery Manufacturers' Federation. He is a medallist of the Franco-British, Brussels, Turin, Venice, and Paris Exhibitions and is the author of two books on pottery: *Art and Craft of the Potter* and *Twentieth Century Ceramics*.

The occasion and the man were well met when he joined the Lancastrian Pottery staff. Two needs were satisfied by that meeting. Iridescent lustre needed a genius to set forth her glory, whilst at large was an artist of genius needing a sphere wherein to employ his extraordinary gifts.

Lustre ware soon felt the impact of his spirit. When one re-members that the Franco-British exhibition was held only two years after his coming to Clifton, it is a remarkable tribute to his genius that several of his pieces exhibited there should be singled out for Special Mention and high praise. A brief description of those pieces appears in Chapter 3, and two other fine examples of his work are described in Chapter 4. But no verbal description can convey the beauty and power of the pieces and of the mind and spirit that produced them. They only need to be seen to be recog-nised as the work of a master. His large pieces are all in private collections but, fortunately, the Manchester Art Galleries Commit-tee have many of his medium-sized pieces. At present, most of these are at their Queen's Park Art Gallery.

Forsyth's photograph depicts the boldness and dash which characterised him and his work. His St. George is no anaemic-looking youth, but vigorous manhood, the impact of whose lance on the fearful-looking dragon was terrific. It was characteristic of him that, when he was in the mood for it, he was a quick worker. His executive skill, combined with aesthetic sensibility, produced work of a high order, in which lettering, heraldic designs, and robust animated figures are prominent features. 'They proclaim their maker's name and do his power display!'

It naturally followed that his studio companions imbibed some-thing of his boldness. Forsyth's indirect influence can be likened to the influence of masters in other walks of life. Sportsmen watching the play of masters in their particular sport acquire a mental picture of their manner of play. The intelligent golfer watching a master play gets enjoyment from it and something else. The re-peated sight of a flowing swing, devoid of jerkiness and with a smooth change of direction at the top, forms in his mind a mental picture. As a result, if in his own efforts mentality habitually influences his play, something of the master's style will pass into his own.

A change in the work of Forsyth's staff was noticeable soon after his arrival. Their freehand work lost its hesitancy, drawing generally and also lettering improved, and their hitherto lifeless forms, both human and animal, took on vitality and purpose.

As he was responsible for everything pertaining to the art side of the ware, he naturally searched for new clay-shapes. His procedure was to sit beside Radford (the thrower) whilst many small pieces were thrown. Radford called these pieces *twifflers* (trifles); Forsyth called them 'sketches in clay' and from them evolved new shapes.

The variety of his work at Clifton, with his consequent growth in experience, helped in no small measure to make him a suitable person for the responsible post of Superintendent of Art Instruction at Stoke-on-Trent, to which he went in 1920. This change located him at the hub of the pottery industry in this country, and thus provided him with a grand opportunity to influence its artistic development. His knowledge of the industry, his experience and skill as an artist craftsman and his keen interest in educational matters, all contributed to his fitness for this wider sphere. His personality expressed itself in these new activities, and it followed as naturally as day follows night that he became the guiding genius of the College of Art.

In his twenty-five years there he sowed the seeds of art in many minds. Some fell on good ground and brought forth fruit, some thirty, some sixty, and some a hundredfold. Many who came under his influence there have filled important and responsible positions, among whom may be mentioned:

Mr. Arthur Barnett, Head of Design Department, Croydon School of Art.

Mr. Leonard Brammer, Supervisor of Arts and Crafts, City of Stoke-on-Trent Education Committee.

Mr. Leonard Butler (now deceased), Formerly Art Teacher.

Mr. Reco Capey, Designer, Messrs. Yardley & Co., London.

Miss Francis Clayton (now Mrs. Ceri Richards), Teacher of Embroidery, Chelsea School of Art.

Miss Clarice Cliffe, Pottery Designer.

Miss Susie Cooper, Susie Cooper Pottery.

Mr. F. Corke, Teacher of Painting and Decorating, Nottingham College of Art.

Mr. Jacob Drew, Principal, Willesden School of Art.

Mr. Arthur Hackney, Part Time Art Teacher.

Mr. Harold Holdcroft, Designer, Messrs. T. C. Wild & Sons.

Mr. Harold Holdway, Designer, Messrs. W. T. Copeland & Sons.

Mr. Thomas B. Jones, Head Designer, Messrs. Pilkingtons' Tiles.

Mr. Arnold Machin, Designer and Sculptor.

Mrs. Constance Marshall, Designer and Illustrator.

Mr. Cecil J. Noke, Art Director, Messrs. Doulton & Sons, Burslem.

Mr. Eric Owen, Modeller, Messrs. Josiah Wedgwood & Sons.

Miss Margaret Owen, Senior Lecturer in Women's Crafts, Ealing School of Art.

Miss Doris Parton, Teacher of Pottery Decoration, Stoke-on-Trent College of Art.

Miss Muriel Pemberton, Dress Design Teacher and Examiner in Art for the Ministry of Education.

Mr. Mark H. Rogers, Art Teacher, St. Joseph's College.

Mr. William Ruscoe, Pottery Teacher, Exeter School of Art.

Mr. Victor Skellern, Art Director, Messrs. Josiah Wedgwood & Sons.

Mr. Eric Slater, Designer, Messrs. Shelley Potteries.

Miss Millicent Taplin, Designer, Messrs. Josiah Wedgwood & Sons.

29. William S. Mycock

30. Richard Joyce

31. Gwladys M. Rodgers

32. John Chambers

33. Kylix
Height 5 in. Dia. 10¼ in.

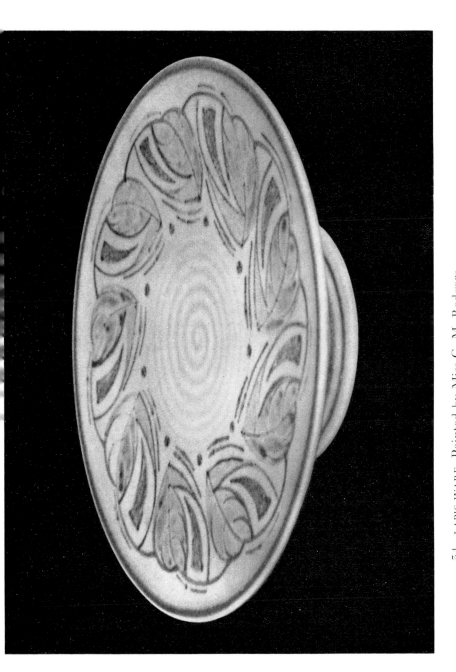

54. LAPIS WARE. Painted by Miss G. M. Rodgers.
Diameter 11 in. Height $2\frac{3}{4}$ in.   *By courtesy of Miss H. Lomax*

55. LAPIS WARE. Painted by Miss G. M. Rodgers.

56. LAPIS WARE. Painted by Miss G. M. Rodgers.   Height 4½ in.
Height 6½ in.
By courtesy of Miss L. Lomax
Author's collection

37. LAPIS WARE. Painted by Miss G. M. Rodgers.

By courtesy of Messrs. Pilkington's Tiles Ltd.

38. Not Lancastrian.
Height 12 in.   *Author's collection*

39. E. T. Radford

40. A. Lomax

Mr. Harold Thomas, Pottery Instructor, Stoke-on-Trent College of Art.

Mr. Frank Trigger, Designer, Messrs. J. & G. Meakin.

The college, in turn, provided him with a wider sphere for the exercise of his exceptional talents. No longer confined to pottery he had ample opportunities to apply his artistic abilities and his fervent spirit to other industrial and cultural arts. 'Gordon Forsyth came to the Potteries as Director of Art Education for the City of Stoke-on-Trent, and it may be worthwhile at this point to pause and consider his work, for quite apart from his designs and decorations for pottery he has exercised a powerful formative influence as a teacher, administrator, and artist. Most of the leading contemporary designers and modellers came under his influence . . . The decorative pottery produced at the insulator factory of Bullers, with superb glazes by Guy Harris, owed much to his enthusiasm, inspiration and guidance. The Susie Cooper Pottery was founded by one of his students. That modern ceramic design is appreciably better today than it was twenty-five years ago is due in no small measure to the efforts which Gordon Forsyth has made on behalf of the industry.'[*]

'Gordon Forsyth did not regard the Art Schools as existing solely to serve the requirements of an industry. He kept before the students the larger ideal of community service, and because of that larger conception of the objects of art education the Art Schools of Stoke-on-Trent have left their impress upon the life of this city. Students have taken part in all sorts of efforts, from the decoration of churches and hospitals to wartime hostels and canteens, nursery schools and civic exhibitions.'[†]

Forty years he was actively associated with the industry, and in that time he wrought so mighty a work that no man can number it. There are several famous names associated with the artistic

[*] *English Country Pottery.*
[†] *A Century of Art Education in the Potteries.* Both by Reginald G. Haggar, R.I.

development of English ceramics. Did any one of them work so mighty a work as did G. M. Forsyth?

He loved pottery. He had a few pieces that he treasured. He showed me three. The first was a piece of Lancastrian lustre. As he handed it to me he said, 'I bought that straight from the kiln. It's one of Charley Cundall's'. He said it in such a way that I sensed, at once, that he was proud of his former pupil and colleague. Then he passed his hand over the piece in that peculiar way that only those who recognise glaze-quality do, and with his face beaming with unalloyed pleasure, he called my attention to the remarkable transparency of its lustre.

His second piece was a superb example of the Sgraffito style of decoration; made of dark red-clay body, coated with a white engobe through which a fine-line design had been incised, and the whole covered with a beautiful turquoise blue glaze. The effect of covering dark red with turquoise made the design appear black. The very delicate design in black under a lovely turquoise made a very beautiful piece full of artistic, technical, and craft charm.

The third piece is the bowl with lion rampant in lustre on a beautiful white porcelain crackled glaze, illustrated in the article 'Potters' Parade' in the trade journal *Pottery and Glass* of 19th October 1949.

His versatility was extraordinary and evidences of it are abundant. Posterity is fortunate in that he has left behind much that enriches our life and at the same time serves as a memorial of him. Among these should be mentioned in addition to the pots he painted, his pictures, and his stained glass windows. One of his latest commissions in windows, perhaps his last, for it was executed in 1951, is in a Methodist Church in Bolton, Lancs. It is a triple group representing the birth, life, and resurrection of Christ. Its rich content of ideas, its fine colour quality and its general effect of a trinity in unity, mark it as the work of a master. He is remembered with gratitude in the Potteries for the murals that once adorned the walls of the Stoke-on-Trent City and General Hospital. During his stay in the hospital, when a serious illness had overtaken him, the sight of the bare walls of the ward and his remembrance that the children's ward had similar bare walls moved him deeply. On his recovery he called together his teachers and senior students, and they voluntarily painted the murals.

What nourished his fertile mind and fruitful life? The answer is not far to seek. He supplied it himself on his retirement from the College of Art at Stoke-on-Trent. In his reply, after a distinguished gathering had expressed by voice and gifts their appreciation of his services, he said, 'We are not here by accident, but by design. Our lives from the day we were born to the day we take our leave, are planned for us'. The simple faith that we are here for the working out of God's purposes was, in him, a 'well of water' springing up, nourishing and inspiring his life. The gifts and graces with which he was so richly endowed at birth he used to work 'the works of Him that sent him'. Full of faith, sure of his powers, fearless and undaunted, he pursued his unwavering course to a triumphant close.

> *Who would true valour see,*
> *Let him come hither;*
> *One here will constant be,*
> *Come wind, come weather;*
>
> *There's no discouragement*
> *Shall make him once relent*
> *His first avowed intent*
> *To be a pilgrim*
>
> *Hobgoblin nor foul fiend*
> *Can daunt his spirit;*
> *He knows he at the end*
> *Shall life inherit.*

JOHN BUNYAN

115

WILLIAM SALTER MYCOCK, J.P.

In the early years of his service he was occupied on the painting of tiles but transferred his activities to pottery when lustre-painting began. This suited his capabilities admirably and he continued to paint lustre ware throughout the whole period of its manufacture. When it was discontinued he retired, having served the company forty-four years, painting lustre ware during thirty of them. No other artist painted lustre for anything like that length of time, so his pieces are far more numerous than those of anyone else.

Mycock's work was not characterised as was Forsyth's, nor as Joyce's. In the main he was dependent on others for ideas and motifs. Where his painting differed from that of the others was in the realm of conventional floral designs and geometric patterns. His work was not entirely confined to lustre for he did some *sgraffito** and incised line decoration and carving of plaques. His work was on a high level and contributed notably to the fame of Lancastrian Pottery. He was awarded a gold medal at the Paris Exhibition of 1925.

His leisure hours were spent in public service. In recognition and in high appreciation of the eminent service thus given he was admitted to be an Honorary Freeman (the first) of the Borough of Swinton and Pendlebury on the 8th of December 1949.

The citation reads: 'Alderman William Salter Mycock is a resident of the Borough, has been a member of the Swinton and Pendlebury Urban District Council for 13 years, a member of the Borough Council for 15 years, Chairman of the Urban District Council 1925-1926, Mayor of the Borough Council 1937-1938, Chairman of the Education Committee from 1927 to 1931 and again from 1934 to 1938; Chairman of the Finance and Office Committee continuously from 1944 up to the present time, and Chairman and Vice-Chairman of other Bodies and Committees, a

* Producing a two-colour design by cutting through a coating of clay of one colour and thereby exposing the colour of the body underneath.

116

Magistrate for the Manchester Petty Sessional Division of the Lancashire County Council from 1929.

'The Council appreciates and acknowledges his many outstanding services to the Borough in various public offices and as representative of the Authority on many Local Government Associations and Bodies, and wishes to express the high esteem in which he is held both by his fellow members and by all citizens of the Borough.

'The Council also desires to place on record its high appreciation of the valuable part played by Alderman Mycock on the advancement of Social Welfare, and in the cultural and industrial life of the Town.'

RICHARD JOYCE

Before coming to Clifton Junction in 1905, Richard Joyce was employed at the Bretby Art Pottery of Messrs. Tooth & Co. Ltd., at Woodville, near Burton-on-Trent, as a painter and designer. He was recommended to William Burton by Bernard Moore. The manner of man he was when young is seen from the fact that he used to walk five miles each way to the Art School at Burton three times per week; there were no public conveyances in those days. It is reported of him by one who was a workmate of his at Woodville, that 'he was a very good workman and a very likeable chap'.

He was a superb craftsman in many branches of the potter's art, having the dexterous, sensitive hand essential for working in clay. Painting, carving, modelling, moulding, and engraving were included in his repertoire. Endowed with such natural gifts and aptitudes and devoted to truthful representation, it is no wonder that his animals are the acme of clay modelling. To see him make a model, then the mould from it, then shape the clay in the mould, and follow that by its withdrawal from the mould and the final touching up was to see craftsmanship at its very best. Much of his leisure was spent studying animal form at the Zoological Gardens at Belle Vue, Manchester. He spent hours and hours there, patiently

117

waiting for animals to assume the attitude he wanted. Fortune sometimes favoured him and the impression was immediately transferred to paper, but often he came away unrewarded. In the studio his birds, animals, and figures were always beautifully drawn and fitted the shape with a natural sense of scale and appreciation of the medium.

A typical example of his style in lustre painting is shown in Plate 13. This cylindrical jar is 6 inches high and 10 inches in circumference. It is coated with an unusual yellow-green glaze which owes its peculiar effect to the pot having been sprayed with Victoria green underglaze pigment before the glaze was applied. The fusion of the glaze caused the dissolution of the pigment, resulting in particles of chromium oxide floating in the glaze. These particles, being unevenly distributed in the glaze, have caused some delicate and lovely variations in tint.

In deep water with waving seaweed and marine animals on the bottom, are seen fishes encircling the piece in seemingly effortless movement, filling the space available without crowding. They are in line formation with heads and tails slightly overlapping. Joyce, by utilising the height of the piece to increase the length of the journey made room for four fishes. They sweep upward and downward in rhythmic movement, smoothly changing direction at the top and bottom. Many other fine examples of his work are shown; three of them designed by other artists and eight designed and painted by him.

Joyce was a quiet, unassuming man with a charming manner, which made him a delightful companion. Blessed with a helpful disposition he readily and willingly placed his wide knowledge of the craft at the service of all. He worked quickly yet was careful and precise in all he did, acting on the principle that 'whatever was worth doing was worth doing well'. He remained at Pilkingtons until his death in 1931. He was awarded a gold medal at the Paris Exhibition in 1925.

CHARLES E. CUNDALL, R.A.

Charles Cundall, born in 1890, came to Clifton Junction in 1907, straight from Ackworth School. He remained until 1914 when he joined the Royal Fusiliers until 1917. He returned to Clifton Junction for a short time and then left to pursue his calling in London.

He came originally to earn money that he might fulfil his ambition to receive training in an Art School. He was happy in his work and in his attendance at evening classes in Manchester, where he was studying for a scholarship to the Royal College of Art in London. William Burton helped him by letting him leave the works early to get to the Art School in the evenings. He holds Mr. Lawrence Pilkington in high regard for his helpful and sympathetic counsel. The few who are left who knew Charles Cundall at Clifton all speak in affectionate terms of him, and are delighted at his successful career since he left them.

His coming to Clifton Junction was an excellent start in his training, for he was immediately under the influence of a unique trio. Moreover, close at hand, was the Manchester School of Art, where he could pursue his studies in the evenings. He had as teacher, adviser, and director, Gordon M. Forsyth. He had as his employer William Burton, who brought him into contact with other artists, facilitated his attendance at the School of Art, and helped him in other ways. And there was Mr. Lawrence Pilkington, a gentleman cultured in the arts to encourage him. Another advantage was that his associates in the studio were kindred spirits. Altogether, he was in a congenial atmosphere which helped him along, lustre ware being an admirable medium for the development of his talent. By hard work and diligence in study, he transformed his opportunity into a stepping stone to higher attainments. Later in life, when he had achieved distinction as a portrait painter, he marked his appreciation of the help he had received from William Burton by painting his portrait. This portrait is in the possession of

119

Mr. Burton's daughter, Mrs. F. C. Ormerod. It is an excellent delineation of the great man.

GWLADYS M. RODGERS

Miss Rodgers was born in Bedale (Yorks.) in 1887. She was the daughter of a Wesleyan Methodist minister. Owing to the peripatetic character of the Methodist ministry, her early education was received at a number of schools, some as far apart as Tredegar and Southport. In the latter town she attended Trinity Hall, which was then a school for the daughters of Wesleyan Methodist ministers. Prior to going to Clifton Junction she received some training in art at the Salford School of Art.

She joined the growing company of artists who were developing a new style of decorative pottery at Pilkingtons' pottery works and in so doing entered upon a highly successful career, for the atmosphere was congenial, stimulating, enthusiastic and encouraging. Her abilities combined with her innate æsthetic sense enabled her to express her ideals through, for her, the eminently suitable medium of pottery painting. In such circumstances she could hardly fail to achieve success. She rose to the occasion and succeeded so well that Royal Lancastrian Pottery now bears her indelible imprint.

Her gifts were expended on lustre until the invention of Lapis decoration in 1928. From then until the manufacture of Lancastrian Pottery ceased in 1938 she confined herself to Lapis ware; indeed she painted practically the whole of it. It owes much of its reputation to her successful adaptation of her style to the new medium. She was skilled at delicate painting, but that was useless for Lapis. It was fortunate that she was resourceful, for it enabled her to adapt her style to meet the need which happened to coincide with her taste. Her work was characterised by originality, freshness, and variety. She was a gold medallist at Paris in 1925.

120

41. Lettered by G. M. Forsyth. Not Lancastrian.

By courtesy of Rt. Rev. Monsignor Browne, P.P.

42. Moulded sweet box lid with very uneven surface. Lettered by G. M. Forsyth. Not Lancastrian.

Length 5 in. Width 3½ in.   *By courtesy of Miss H. Lomax*

43. Lettered by G. M. Forsyth.
Diameter 9½ in. Height 4 in.

44. An exhibition piece. Inscription AMOR NON CONOSCE TRAVAGLIO ('Love is Unaware of Toil') is painted on a concave surface on a band 1⅛ in. wide. On the lady's hairband is an inscription AMOR VIN CIT OMNIA ('Love Conquers all things'). Details of the lady's dress—the waviness of her hair, the rings upon her fingers, are all picked out in beautiful lustre. Painted by G. M. Forsyth.

Height 3½ in. Inside depth 2¼ in. Diameter 10 in.   *Author's collection*

45. Painted by G. M. Forsyth.
Height 9½ in.   *By courtesy of Manchester Art Galleries Committee*

46. Painted by G. M. Forsyth.
Height 15 in.

Author's collection

47. When exhibited in Berlin before the first world war this piece interested Kaiser Wilhelm II. He asked the price but did not buy. Were the inscriptions not to his liking? Painted by G. M. Forsyth.
Height 12 in.
By courtesy of Mr. Arthur Chambers.

AMOR GIGNET AMOREM
('Love begets love')

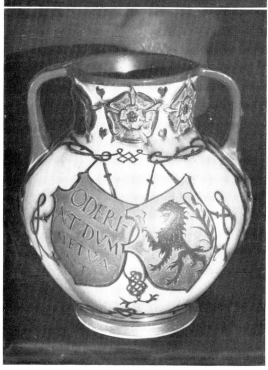

ODERINT DUM METUANT
('Let them hate provided that they fear')

Height 10¾ in.

Height 10 in.

49. Painted by G. M. Forsyth. Considered to be one of the firm's master-pieces.
Height 10 in.

Author's collection

50. Painted by G. M. Forsyth. QVI NON LABORET NON MANDVCET ('If a man
does not work, let him not eat')

Height 9¾ in.　　　*By courtesy of Manchester Art Galleries Committee*

51. Painted by R. Joyce.
Height 9½ in.

Author's collection

52. Painted by R. Joyce.
Height 8½ in. plus cover

53. Carved by R. Joyce. Eggshell surface glaze.
Height 10½ in.   *By courtesy of Mrs. L. A. Pettiner*

54. Painted by R. Joyce. An excellent example of lustre ware on an opalescent glaze showing Joyce's skill in depicting animal form. There are three leopards and all are beautifully drawn.

Height 10 in.
By courtesy of Mr. W. Bray

55. Three pieces painted by W. S. Mycock.

By courtesy of Manchester Art Galleries Committee

Height 7 in. *Author's collection*

Height 5½ in.

56. Both painted by W. S. Mycock

57. Incised by W. S.
Mycock. Glossy
matt glaze, orange
red ship, etc. Brown
background, etc.
Diameter 17 in.
*By courtesy of
Mr. J. H. Lomax*

58. Incised by
W. S. Mycock.
White seagulls
outlined in dark blue
on a very pale
greenish blue
background.
Eggshell glaze.
Diameter $11\frac{1}{4}$ in.
*By courtesy of
Mr. W. Lomax*

59. Painted by W. S. Mycock.
Height 5¼ in. Diameter 8 in.   *By courtesy of Mrs. W. G. Boustead*

60. Painted by W. S. Mycock.
Height 5¼ in. Diameter 13½ in.   *Author's collection*

CHAPTER 11

Craftsmen

Meaning those workers who shaped pottery by hand.

'So every carpenter and workmaster, that laboureth night and day: and they that cut and grave seals, and are diligent to make great variety: the smith also sitting by the anvil, and his eyes look still upon the pattern of the thing he maketh; he setteth his mind to finish his work, and watcheth to polish it perfectly: So doth the potter sitting at his work, and turning the wheel about with his feet, who is alway carefully set at his work, and maketh all his work by number; He fashioneth the clay with his arm, and boweth down his strength before his feet; he applieth himself to lead it over; and he is diligent to make clean the furnace: All these trust to their hands: and everyone is wise in his work.

'Without these cannot a city be inhabited: and they shall not dwell where they will, nor go up and down: They shall not be sought for in publick counsel, nor sit high in the congregation: they shall not sit on the judges' seat, nor understand the sentence of judgement; and they shall not be found where parables are spoken. But they will maintain the state of the world, and (all) their desire is in the work of their craft.'

ECCLESIASTICUS

THE FIRST CRAFTSMAN to be employed in making Lancastrian Pottery was *Robert Tunnicliffe*, who started in 1897. He was an excellent workman, skilled at pottery-making by several methods.

The next, *William Bray*, started fresh from school at thirteen years of age. He was the firm's first apprentice and was put to learn the trade with Tunnicliffe, who made the lad into a good workman, expert at pressing, casting, mould-making, and fashioning pots on a whirler. He learned much, too, from E. T. Radford, the thrower, but his greatest teacher and the one who most powerfully shaped his craftsmanship, was that master artist-potter, Richard Joyce.

Bray continued in the service of the firm for over fifty years.

Both Tunnicliffe and Bray were potting for some years before a potter's wheel was installed at the works. When that time arrived, an additional presser named *John Clunn* was engaged. Apart from the thrower, these three were the chief potters in the early years.

THROWER. Pilkingtons were exceptionally fortunate when, in answer to an advertisement in the *Staffordshire Sentinel*, *Edward Thomas Radford* applied for the position of *thrower*. Though at the time of his application he was 'off the wheel', having spent some years in other work, he was, nevertheless, in the prime of life and the fullness of skill, with a high reputation as a thrower, especially as a thrower of large pots.

Thus it came about that when the first potter's wheel at Clifton Junction began to revolve on 30th November 1903, E. T. Radford sat at it and began the shaping of pots that have delighted their owners in many lands. He remained with Pilkingtons until his retirement in 1936. He died in August 1937, aged 77 years. His skill and his enthusiasm for his craft remained with him to the end.

He began his connection with the pottery trade in 1873 when he was indentured with Messrs. Josiah Wedgwood & Sons, of Etruria, Staffordshire. The indenture was for a period of seven years. It was signed by himself, his father, and Mr. Francis Wedgwood and stipulated that he must be indoors by 10 p.m. His father had to guarantee his good behaviour when away from the works. He worked for a time on the original *string* wheel whereon Josiah Wedgwood worked when he made his own pottery. There was also an earlier type of wheel, known as a *kick* wheel, which the apprentices had to work as punishment for misbehaviour; young Radford often had to work on this wheel. As its speed was much slower and he was on piecework his wages suffered in consequence.

He completed his apprenticeship in 1880 and was successful in obtaining the post on the head wheel at a newly opened pottery at

Linthorpe, near Middlesbrough, Yorks., where a very wide range of 'art' ware, stamped 'Linthorpe', was made. Here he gained experience in making large pieces, some vases being 36 inches high when fired. He left this factory in 1886 and went to Burmantofts, a branch of the Leeds Fireclay Co. Ltd., to make 'big stuff' for them. From here he moved to Messrs. Doulton, at Lambeth, where he also made special lines of big ware. He did not remain long at Lambeth, for Messrs. Wedgwood invited him to return and make large pieces for them. Here William Burton first met him and often watched him throwing. So it doubtless greatly rejoiced his heart when he read Radford's application.

He was a very obliging workman. For several years it was part of my duties to take visitors round the works, so I had ample opportunities of observing him. Whatever he was doing when visitors arrived, and no matter whether it was convenient or not, he always graciously received us. He laid aside what he was doing and proceeded to enthrall us with a fine exhibition of skill in this fascinating craft.

Among the things he did for the delectation of his visitors there were usually three which never failed to impress them as exhibitions of marvellous skill. He would throw a good sized pot; then by means of a fine wire would cut it in halves vertically to show how uniformly thick was the wall of the piece. Another pot he would fashion with a circular rebated opening in the top. This he would put on one side whilst he made a lid like a teapot lid for it. When the lid was transferred to the pot it would fit perfectly, no other measuring instrument than the human eye being used. His third demonstration would be to throw a wide shallow bowl with sloping sides. Then, with the knuckle of his first finger, he would make a continuous series of circles gradually and evenly extending from centre to circumference.

And while he plied his magic art—
For it was magical to me—

123

I stood in silence and apart,
And wondered more and more to see
That shapeless, lifeless mass of clay
Rise up to meet the master's hand,
And now contract and now expand,
And e'en his slightest touch obey.

KERAMOS

Radford was certainly most highly skilled at the craft, whether throwing extreme sizes or average pieces. To watch him at work was a privilege and a delightful experience, for he presented a picture of masterful ease and graceful movement. He was, indeed, a great artist on the wheel, and his fame spread far and wide.

He was a versatile craftsman on the wheel, expert in turning as well as in throwing; he was equally at home with pots large and small, thick and thin, smooth or finger finished. In the possession of his son is a bulbous vase complete with shaped rim and foot, standing only a quarter of an inch high, with the other dimensions in keeping. It was thrown and turned by Radford on the wheel. All thrown shapes were in his province, be they single or multiple curved. His raised circles on the inside of trays and the spirals on his finger-finished vases bear the strictest examination. He always appeared to be at ease and master of the job in hand. He was happy in his work and looked it. He was a craftsman—thrower and turner *par excellence*, and was justly renowned as the finest thrower of his time.

Appropriating those lovely lines of 'George Eliot' about Stradivari and his violins to Radford and his vases we get:

. . . *When any mortal holds*
Twixt hand and eye a thrown vase of mine
He will be glad that E. T. Radford lived
Made vases and made them of the best,
. . . *'Tis God gives skill,*
But not without men's hands: He could not make

124

Edward T. Radford's vases
Without Edward Radford.

It is interesting to note in connection with both his skill on the wheel and his ability to shape exceptionally small pieces, that his son, who also was a thrower at Pilkingtons for some years, also acquired a good reputation as a thrower, and his grandson is a specialist in ophthalmic surgery, where his gift for dealing sensitively with very minute things has a special value.

Radford, with his long experience, felt being confined to shapes drawn for him somewhat irksome. He knew the capabilities and responsiveness of clay and the capabilities and responsiveness of his fingers. He had the right feeling for clay. A lump of plastic clay was a pot in embryo to him. Having confidence in himself he desired liberty to produce his own shapes. William Burton and Gordon Forsyth agreed that he should have this liberty. Both of them often sat beside him, encouraging him and making suggestions, all the while thrilled by his graceful and poetic movements. This liberation from bondage expanded his usefulness and deepened his impress on the ware.

For the greater part of his time his wheel was revolved by means of a rope and rope-pulley turned by one man if the pot was small, and by two if large; and by a young woman when he was turning the semi-dry shapes. All the clay he used was wedged by hand; no pug mill, or air extractor was ever used.

He did not sign his pieces until near the end of his time, so there are not many of these signed pieces. All were fired together in the last biscuit oven before he left. They have his initials scratched legibly on the base. Some of them were not glazed until the last glazing kiln of Lancastrian Pottery in 1938. These are marked on the base 'March 1938'.

OTHER WORKMEN

Harold Thomas was engaged as additional thrower in 1927 on the recommendation of Gordon M. Forsyth, and continued with the firm until making ceased ten years afterwards. Throwing was, and still is, a continual delight to him, for he is conscious of an inborn sense of clay value and forms appropriate to it. He greatly admired Radford's work and the masterly way it was done. Since leaving Pilkingtons he has been at the Stoke-on-Trent College of Art, where he is a full-time pottery instructor.

In 1932 *John Brennan* was apprenticed to throwing and began his career under Radford. He remained until the cessation of manufacture in 1938.

For a short time before production ceased a young potter named Spencer modelled figures and groups.

William Brockbank was the principal glaze sprayer. He followed that occupation for about thirty years until the manufacture of Lancastrian Pottery was discontinued in 1938. For some years before being put to glaze spraying he was my assistant in the lead house, where he acquired a good knowledge of glazes, and particularly of their working qualities.

To the outsider, glaze-spraying seems a simple operation not calling for much skill; therein it is deceptive. The fact is that the sprayed work of others was not equal to his. They watched him; they asked how he did it; he told them and showed them; they tried to produce his results but failed. It may be that his previously acquired knowledge of the working properties of glazes gave him an advantage. But he had that indefinable something called 'the knack of it'. He seemed to have an innate sense of the concentration of particles required. He had judgment of the thickness of deposit needed, and of the thickness of the layer whilst it was being built up. Above all, he was clever in manipulating the process, and that, for the best results, requires great skill.

He was a trustworthy assistant, a workman interested in his job, well liked by his workmates and a delightful companion. He took a deep interest in his work and rejoiced greatly at his success. Royal Lancastrian Pottery owes much to his masterly technique for producing speckled, mottled and other texture glazes, and especially for the remarkable texture that he gave to the famous 'Kingfisher blue' and Orange-Vermilion glazes. In his leisure hours violin playing was his recreation.

CHAPTER 12

The Chemist's Activities

Chemist: Abraham Lomax

In FEBRUARY 1896, I accepted the invitation to leave the office desk to become the works assistant to Joseph Burton. My duties were, first, to keep all departments supplied with clays, glazes and colours of constant composition and working properties. Secondly, to deal with the technological problems that arose from day to day. Thirdly, to make any experiments needed by my chiefs and associates and lastly, to use what time was available in making such experiments as seemed good to me to make. With the passage of time I became more and more acquainted with all the technological aspects of manufacture, from the raw materials—their sources, composition, properties and suitability—through all stages of manufacture and behaviour to the final product. Though at no time had I any responsibility for any part of the designing, shaping, firing, glazing, decorating and commercial departments, my work, of necessity, brought me into close contact with all of them, as they were all in one way or another affected by it. My relations with the heads of other departments were most cordial and our collaboration mutually helpful. Thus I acquired a comprehensive and thorough knowledge of the processes and productions of the firm.

Very early in my new work Joseph Burton taught me how to make experiments. One of the very earliest series I did under his instructions and supervision resulted in the discovery of a beauti-fully smooth eggshell glaze. This discovery was fortunate and timely, for architects were pressing for a better surface for interior wall tiling than the glassy-faced tiles then in use. This discovery enabled the company to begin immediately the industrial production of smooth matt glazed tiles. Thus they were the pioneers of a practice soon followed by others and which has since been developed to an enormous extent.

As my experimental methods gradually won the confidence of both William and Joseph Burton they soon allowed me to proceed on my own lines, and thus it came about that, owing to my being possessed of or by an insatiable curiosity and my having become well versed in chemistry, from 1901 by far the greater part of the 16,000 trials I made were 'off my own bat'. This explains how it came about that many of the important discoveries mentioned on page 152 were initiated and carried through by me.

It should be mentioned that there was also a laboratory chemist employed. *Norman Sinclair* was the first to occupy that position. He served the firm from November 1898 to November 1906. He was mainly occupied with the usual type of work done in works laboratories, such as the routine testing of raw materials, the making of analyses and measurements of solubilities and clay contractions, etc., as well as theoretical investigations. In addition to these matters he made glaze-experiments for William and Joseph Burton. These glaze-experiments were quite independent of those I was making, though at times they were of a similar character.

Our knowledge of experimental work done previous to 1901 is very scanty indeed. No written records of experiments by William Burton in that period have been preserved, nor have any of his later work. The only experimental work of Joseph Burton on record is that in his Presidential address to the English Ceramic Society, wherein he described his experiments in 1893 with chromate of iron in a lead glaze, and some experiments he made after I left, which he recorded on pages unused by me in my last note book. Only odd items of my earlier work have been kept, but fortunately the records of my experiments in the period 1901-1911 have been preserved. All my note books of that period, numbered consecutively 1-24, are in the firm's possession. They are rich in interesting and serviceable information and I have referred to them for the purposes of this book.

One very important set of experiments was made in the last century. It was concerned with the change over from 'raw' lead glazes to 'fritted' lead glazes. The change was the outcome of a serious agitation in the country concerning lead poisoning in the pottery industry. Raw lead glazes contained white lead, a material which possessed great flotative power. However long a glaze liquid had been standing unused it was easily stirred up and made ready for use. The change to fritted lead, i.e., lead oxide fused with china clay, flint, etc., altered all this. Glaze-liquids containing such frit '*set*' badly. The glaze materials settled to the bottom of the container and formed a sticky mass which was difficult to stir up and re-suspend properly. How to avoid this was a problem. Knowing that a small amount of alkali added to a clay slip* would make the slip more fluid and thus less water or more clay would give the same consistency, it occurred to me that possibly some other water soluble substance might do the opposite and thicken a glaze liquid and thus prevent 'setting'. In the lead-house were a dozen or so water-soluble substances. I put a pint of glaze in some basins, added to each of them a small amount of soluble material—one substance only per basin—then stirred the mixtures well and allowed them to settle overnight. Next morning all but the one which contained calcium chloride had set. Henceforth, the setting of glazes was avoided by adding a little calcium chloride. That is an example of the 'hit or miss' method of experiment. It nearly missed! William Burton passed the information on to the potters in North Staffordshire, for they were experiencing the same trouble.

The four years, 1901-1904, were years of intense experimental

* A thick fluid consisting of clay and water.

130

activity. Many lines of experiments were running concurrently. There were trials for Flambé, Crystalline, Opalescent, and Alkaline (Persian) glazes. In addition, two entirely new coloured glazes were produced.

The flambé and crystalline glaze experiments derived their stimulus from the Paris Exhibition of 1900. On his return from Paris, William Burton started trials for both. He directed the flambé experiments from start to finish. He supplied the initial ideas for the experiments on crystalline glazes and later left me to pursue them on my own lines. The other four were initiated by me and carried through, from start to finish, by me.

In judging the potter, it should always be borne in mind that there are definite limitations within which he works. One is the stern law that 'the clay determines the pot'. The Old Testament story of Jeremiah's visit to the potter's house well illustrates this. He saw the potter throwing a vessel; the attempt failed. A second attempt succeeded because he fashioned *another* vessel. It is probable that his clay came from a local clay pit, and, unlike the clay used by modern potters, was not of uniform consistency; some portions may have been stiffer than the rest and resisted the pressure of the potter's thumb and fingers, preventing him making a perfectly shaped pot. Hence, he squeezed the clay together again and made something within the capability of the clay, maybe some common article like a bowl or a shallow dish.

Clay determines size, shape, colour, modelling, character and consequent colour of glaze, and finally, the artist's decoration. Truly 'the clay determines the pot'.

All the experiments made by me, whether on a small or large scale, were works experiments and had to conform to works conditions. The manufacture of coloured decorative pottery was being grafted on to a works making tiles. The plastic clay that would be used for throwing vases would be fired in ovens with firing conditions suited to compressed clay-dust tiles, and the new glazes that would be applied must mature in the firing conditions appropriate to glazed tiles. No other firing conditions were available in my time.

The force of these limitations was not felt or recognised at the time. Viewed after the lapse of half a century their cramping effect is plainly seen. To take one aspect only, that of the area of firing conditions available; this was limited to three regions. (1) That of a majolica glaze kiln (1,000°-1,050°C.); (2) that of a glost oven (1,050°-1,100°C.); and (3) that of a biscuit oven (1,200°-1,250°C.). The duration of the firing remained unaltered. Nowadays the modern electrically-heated ovens will provide any desired temperature up to 1,300°C., and the firing can be kept at any chosen temperature for any length of time desired. Remembering the many hours that our majolica kilns were fired, it is astonishing to learn that, today enamellers can fuse and mature the second coat of enamel in so short a time as three minutes! As regards precision of temperature, I have recently seen pottery the glaze of which is coloured by a previously prepared pigment which can only be made if the temperature does not vary more than $+$ or $-$ 10°C. Such precision of heat-treatment was unthought of in the potteries of fifty years ago. The coming of the electrically-heated firing chamber has revealed how rigidly circumscribed were our activities.

Some of the results of this experimental work appear in this book; many do not, for they would not add to the story of Lancastrian Pottery, even though the record of the experiments would provide interesting reading. For instance, I say nothing about experiments for alkaline glazes of the type used by the Persian and Syrian potters, though a thousand were made, because, though we were highly successful with them on tiles, our attempts to apply them to pottery were only partially successful. However, I think I ought to mention one result in order to correct a common misapprehension. It has been frequently stated that lead is an unsuitable material for such glazes as it turns the blue colour of turquoise to green. That can easily happen, but a glaze containing nearly 20% of lead oxide gave a superb turquoise-blue equal to the best blue in glazes free from lead. To do this it is essential to cease the firing immediately maturity is reached. Readers will have noticed that discoveries came about in various ways. On page 130 is the story of a very useful discovery made by the 'hit or miss' method, whereas page 62 describes one resulting from the exactly opposite method of searching by methodical experiments. Then on page 26 there is the story of a mishap that led to a succession of most extraordinary results, and below is the account of one which I can only describe as being due to *intuition*.

A most unusual way, indeed it is the only one of its sort that I remember having occurred to me personally, was that of a sudden vivid flash of inspiration. It happened at a time when we were experiencing serious trouble and much financial loss owing to coloured majolica glazes ruckling during firing, leaving the glaze slightly uneven in thickness, with consequent unevenness of colour. One night, when not thinking about the matter at all, it suddenly flashed into my mind that the cause of the trouble might be ferrous sulphate contamination of the oxide of iron we used for colouring some of the glazes. The oxide we used was the purple oxide resulting from the calcination of ferrous sulphate, and if it was not thoroughly washed after calcination it would be so contaminated. In those early days we did not test materials before using them. We always used them in the condition 'as bought', never having thought such a precaution as testing to be necessary. A test was immediately made and showed the oxide to be so contaminated and thus the cause of our trouble. Whence came that flash? 'The wind bloweth where it listeth, and thou hearest the sound thereof, but canst not tell whence it cometh, and whither it goeth.'

I trust that these few pages will have given the reader some indication of the atmosphere in which my work was done. I see now, but did not at the time, how fortunate I was in having such a rare opportunity amidst most favourable circumstances. It was a great experience to work with such colleagues as those described in the previous three chapters and also with competent departmental heads and skilled workers, all of us under the guidance of William and Joseph Burton. Throughout it all I had full liberty to follow my own bent.

It was a great privilege to be allowed full liberty to travel life's pathway as it opened out before me. No restrictions whatever hampered the outpouring of my individuality. To me it was given to enjoy the ampler, purer air of freedom. I was fortunate also in the time of my service, for I was exploring virgin ground containing treasures of great value, some of which I had the good fortune to unearth. These were great advances and the Art of the Potter has been enriched thereby.

The foregoing gives some indication of my part in the rise and development of Lancastrian Pottery. William Burton, in the presence of his brother Joseph, said to me a few days before I left the firm, 'You have left your impress on the productions of the firm'. Nobody will dispute his competence to judge.

I must add, in all sincerity, that I do not count myself to have done anything worthy of a place in the ranks of human achievement. Discovery has many epic stories of human effort, but there is nothing worthy of special commendation about mine. These successes cost me nothing. I only looked about me when no one else was troubling to look and found great treasures lying close to hand. It happened as Job predicted when he said 'Speak to the earth and it shall teach thee' (Job XII, 8).

> *O Lord, how manifold are thy works!*
> *In wisdom hast thou made them all:*
> *The Earth is full of thy riches.*

It is, of course, a great satisfaction to me to have done these things. I marvel that it should have fallen to my lot to enrich life by bringing into view these wondrous beauties. The credit is HIS who gave me a talent and appointed me my task.

Lancastrian Pottery's
Indebtedness
to Science

CHAPTER 13

Contributions by Science

NATURE'S STOREHOUSE

Eᴀʀʟʏ ɪɴ ᴛʜᴇ ɴɪɴᴇᴛᴇᴇɴᴛʜ century, John Dalton put forward some views concerning the atom. Later, these became crystallised into what is known as Dalton's Atomic Theory. This theory served as a working hypothesis and by it the structure of modern chemistry was built. About the middle of the century chemists began to doubt the accuracy of the atomic weights then being used in chemical calculations. In consequence, eminent chemists set about the exacting task of obtaining more accurate ones. As these new atomic weights became available a few chemists in different countries, notably Newlands here in England in 1863, Mendeléeff in Russia in 1869, and Lothar Meyer in Germany in 1871 observed that some of the chemical elements could be grouped in families; the members of these families having similar properties.

The history of science has many instances of the gradual accumulation of facts and observations which, for a time, seem unrelated; then, first one and later other workers, detect indications of order. These ideas are spread and pondered and eventually a seer appears and clarifies matters by a generalisation which co-ordinates the whole into a comprehensive orderly scheme. The idea of gravitational attraction occurred to several people including Halley and Wren in this country; then Isaac Newton appeared and gave the idea form and substance.

Similarly, the idea of an orderly relationship of atomic weight to properties simmered in men's minds in the 1860's. The seer with

136

penetrating vision soon appeared in the person of Dimitri Ivan-ovitsch Mendeléeff, a Russian chemist. He arranged and rearranged the elements in tables. His last arrangement appeared in 1871. In this table the elements are placed in the order of their atomic weights in horizontal rows in octaves; the rows being placed under each other with the lightest elements in the top row and the heaviest at the bottom. The elements were thus grouped both horizontally and vertically. This arrangement is known as *The Periodic Table of the Elements* and is reproduced overleaf.

This grouping gave to chemists a new power of great potency. By means of it, chemistry made great strides forward, especially in understanding the constitution of the matter of which the universe is made. The modern arrangement is designed to display quite other relationships between the atoms and so differs from the earlier form. It is this earlier form that interests potters, for that arrangement reveals that elements possessing some similar properties happen to fall into the same vertical column. Many elements were unknown then; hence the gaps in the table. (All are now known).

Here are some groups of elements found in the same vertical columns, all of which are used by the potter.

COLUMN	ELEMENTS	OXIDES
I	Copper, Silver, Gold	
I	Lithium, Sodium, Potassium	R_2O
II	Calcium, Strontium, Barium	RO
II	Magnesium, Zinc, Cadmium	RO
III	Boron, Aluminium	R_2O_3
IV	Silicon, Titanium, Zirconium, Tin	RO_2

I was intensely interested in this periodic table. It made a powerful impression on me. I revelled in Mendeléeff's 'Principles of Chemistry' for it was a superb treatise on the subject. I read and studied it with avidity, and, in consequence, became steeped in knowledge of the similarities of elements in the vertical columns. The table

137

was a fine tool for me, and I made great use of it and was rewarded beyond my expectations. It led me to think that elements might be substituted for others; for instance, that strontia or baryta could replace lime, since all three are in the same vertical column, and that zinc could replace magnesia and, possibly lime. Of course, I was well aware that no two elements are alike in all respects and therefore I should probably find some differences in the products of such substitutions. It was these differences that I sought to find,

PERIODIC TABLE OF LATE

(Atomic weights to

Series	1	2	3	4 RH₄
Group	R₂O	RO	R₂O₃	RO₂
I	Hydrogen 1			
II	Lithium 7	Beryllium 9	Boron 11	Carbon 12
III	Sodium 23	Magnesium 24	Aluminium 27	Silicon 28
IV	Potassium 39	Calcium 40	Scandium 44	Titanium 50
V	Copper 63	Zinc 65	Gallium 69	?
VI	Rubidium 85	Strontium 87	Yttrium 89	Zirconium 89
VII	Silver 108	Cadmium 112	Indium 113	Tin 118
VIII	Caesium 133	Barium 137	Lanthanum 139	Cerium 140
IX	?	?	?	?
X	?	?	Ytterbium 173	?
XI	Gold 196	Mercury 200	Thallium 204	Lead 207
XII	?	?	?	Thorium 233

This table is from "Experimental Proofs of Chemical Theory"

138

and the search for them led to great discoveries.

Very many substitution experiments were made extending over several years wherein elements of a particular class were replaced by others of the same class, and much valuable information was gained thereby. In the R_2O class when potash replaced sodium in alkaline glaze frits the frits were less fusible, less resistant to atmospheric disintegration and gave glazes which crazed worse. No substitution experiments were made with elements in the

NINETEENTH CENTURY DATE

nearest whole number)

5 RH_3 R_2O_5	6 RH_2 RO_3	7 RH R_2O_7	8 R_2H RO_4
Nitrogen 14	Oxygen 16	Fluorine 19	
Phosphorus 31	Sulphur 32	Chlorine 35	
Vanadium 51	Chromium 52	Manganese 54	Cobalt 59 Iron 56
Arsenic 75	Selenium 79	Bromine 80	Nickel 58
Niobium 94	Molybdenum 96	?	Ruthenium 104 Rhodium 104
Antimony 120	Tellurium 128	Iodine 127	Palladium 106
Didymium 147	?	?	
Erbium 166	?	?	Iridium 193
Tantalum 182	Wolfram 184	?	Platinum 194
Bismuth 210	?	?	Osmium 199
?	Uranium 238	?	

by William Ramsay, Ph.D., 1884.

139

R_2O_3 class. In the RO_2 class the oxides of titanium, zirconium and titanium were opacifiers* and so were antimony, arsenic and phosphorus oxides of the R_2O_5 class. In that class vanadium sometimes gave iridescence as does bismuth.

But it was the experiments made with oxides of the RO group which yielded the most interesting and profitable results. As early as 1901 systematic experiments were made to determine if the substitution of other oxides caused any difference in the shade of the turquoise colour of alkaline glazes. Using lime (CaO) as the standard for comparison, it was replaced wholly by other RO oxides in turn; these being strontia (SrO), baryta (BaO), magnesia (MgO), and zinc (ZnO). Frits were made according to the formula $0 \cdot 75$ Na_2O, $0 \cdot 25$ RO, $2 \cdot 00$ SiO_2. These frits were ground and to each was added some oxide of copper and the mixture applied to tiles as a glaze. The effect on the turquoise colour was nil, for all were identical. Other differences, however, were noticed. The magnesia glaze was the least fusible and the baryta glaze the most fusible; and these two glazes differed from the rest in being more susceptible to atmospheric decomposition.

If the firing of a glaze is stopped before maturity is reached, chemical action is arrested and any undissolved material retains something of its own characteristics. Many matt glazes are produced in this way. Three such matt glazes were made, one with an excess of lime, a second with an excess of magnesia, and a third with an excess of zinc oxide. Colouring oxides and pigments were added to each. The results are shown on the table which follows. There are some striking differences.

John Dalton's work stands, and so does that of Dimitri Mendeléeff. Their names will remain among the immortals, for they helped men to understand some of the mysteries of the atom.

* Mr. Norman Sinclair, who has had over fifty years experience with glazes of many kinds, informs me that oxides of titanium, zirconium, and tin, like silica in the same group, all reduce crazing.

COLOUR CHANGES DUE TO SUBSTITUTIONS
IN MATT GLAZES

Colouring Material	Colour in Lime Glaze	Colour in Magnesia Glaze	Colour in Zinc Glaze
1. Oxide of Nickel	Dull Brown to Dull Green	Light Drab	Greyish Blue
2. Oxide of Cobalt	Dull Blue	Weak Lilac	Brilliant Blue
3. Oxide of Iron	Weak Yellow to Brown	Purer than lime gives	Much stronger colour than the other two glazes give
4. Oxide of Chromium	Grass Green	Greyish Green	Greyish Blue
5. Oxide of Copper	Green	Slightly yellower than lime gives	Slightly bluer colour than the other two glazes give
6. Oxide of Manganese	Purplish Brown	Purplish Brown	Purplish Brown
7. Chromate of Iron	Dull Green	Dull Green	Terra-Cotta
8. Chromate of Copper	Nearly the same as No. 5	Slightly bluer than lime gives	Dark Greenish Grey
9. Sodium Uranate	Dull Orange Brown	Dull Orange Brown	Dull Orange Brown
10. Rutile	Almost Colourless	Orange Brown	Cream to Dull Yellow
11. Crimson Stain	Good Crimson	Heliotrope	Duller Heliotrope than Magnesia glaze
12. Underglaze Yellow	Rich Yellow	Rich Yellow	Weaker and duller than others

Behind the Periodic Table is the Mind that designed the atom, that spaced its electrons in cycles, appointed them their places, and endowed them with power. Gratitude should be the constant companion of the potter, for, just as the musician, playing on the keys of the organ, elicits Nature's harmonies of sound to delight his ear and rest his soul, so the potter, playing on the keyboard of the Periodic Table, evokes Nature's harmonies of colour to delight his eye and charm his mind.

AN EXAMPLE OF SYSTEMATIC RESEARCH

At the turn of the century the pottery industry was woefully lacking in fundamental knowledge concerning the properties of its raw materials and of their individual values to the potter. Pottery works had built up their recipes by empirical methods and were reluctant to make changes because of uncertainty as to what might happen. 'Better leave well alone' was their motto. If a potter was experiencing trouble with his glaze he had no sound basis to work upon to find out the cause of his trouble or the cure for it. His trials, therefore, were more or less empirical in character. There was a pressing need for definite reliable information about the functions of glaze components.

One of the most important glaze components is alumina. It is a constituent of most of the commonly used glazes, and though it has been widely used for centuries no one appears to have had anything approaching a thorough knowledge of its functions and capabilities. Hence it provided a fine target for investigation.

A series of experiments consisting of gradual increases in the alumina content of three widely different types of glazes was made in the hope that they would elucidate the mystery. The three types chosen were (1) Glazes made from lead silicates, (2) Simple leadless boro-silicate glazes, (3) Complex lead glazes. The experiments with type 2 are detailed in Tables 1-5 showing their systematic and comprehensive character. The results exceeded expectations.

Type 2

ADDITIONS OF ALUMINA AND SILICA TO DIBASIC BORO-SILICATE

Table No. 1

No.	*Molecular Composition*					*Results*
	Na_2O	CaO	Al_2O_3	B_2O_3	SiO_2	E.F. Majolica Kiln
1	0·75	0·25	0·00	0·67	2·00	Transparent. Very uneven.
2	,,	,,	0·10	,,	,,	Unevenness gradually diminish-
3	,,	,,	0·20	,,	,,	ing with increase of alumina.
4	,,	,,	0·30	,,	,,	Slight characteristic alkaline scum.
5	,,	,,	0·40	,,	,,	
6	,,	,,	0·50	,,	,,	Good transparent glaze.
7	,,	,,	0·70	,,	,,	Not properly fused.
8	,,	,,	0·80	,,	,,	
9	,,	,,	0·90	,,	,,	Badly blibbed.
10	,,	,,	1·00	,,	,,	
11	,,	,,	0·00	,,	2·33	Uneven transparent glaze.
12	,,	,,	0·10	,,	,,	No alkaline scum.
13	,,	,,	0·20	,,	,,	
to			to			Good transparent glaze.
17	,,	,,	0·60	,,	,,	
18	,,	,,	0·70	,,	,,	Not properly matured.
19	,,	,,	0·80	,,	,,	Not matured. Blibbed.
20	,,	,,	0·90	,,	,,	Not matured. Blibbed. Slight dry edge.
21	,,	,,	1·00	,,	,,	Semi-fused. Blibbed.
22	,,	,,	0·00	,,	2·67	Unlevel transparent glaze.
23	,,	,,	0·10	,,	,,	Unlevel transparent glaze.
24	,,	,,	0·20	,,	,,	
to			to			Good transparent glaze.
28	,,	,,	0·60	,,	,,	
29	,,	,,	0·70	,,	,,	Pinholy transparent glaze.
30	,,	,,	0·80	,,	,,	Not properly matured.
31	,,	,,	0·90	,,	,,	Semi-fused.
32	,,	,,	1·00	,,	,,	Semi-fused.

Type 2

ADDITIONS OF ALUMINA AND SILICA TO DIBASIC BORO-SILICATE

Table No. 2

No.	Molecular Composition					Results
	Na_2O	CaO	Al_2O_3	B_2O_3	SiO_2	E.F. Majolica Kiln
1	0·67	0·33	0·00	0·67	2·00	Uneven transparent glaze.
2	,,	,,	0·10	,,	,,	Transparent glaze slightly uneven.
3	,,	,,	0·20	,,	,,	Transparent glaze slightly uneven.
4	,,	,,	0·30	,,	,,	Transparent glaze.
5	,,	,,	0·40	,,	,,	Good transparent glaze.
6	,,	,,	0·50	,,	,,	Good transparent glaze.
7	,,	,,	0·60	,,	,,	Transparent glaze not quite matured.
8	,,	,,	0·70	,,	,,	Not properly fused.
9	,,	,,	0·80	,,	,,	Badly blibbed.
10			to			
11	,,	,,	1·00	,,	,,	Badly blibbed.
12	,,	,,	0·00	,,	2·33	Good transparent glaze.
13	,,	,,	0·10	,,	,,	
14	,,	,,	0·20	,,	,,	
15	,,	,,	0·30	,,	,,	Excellent transparent glaze.
16	,,	,,	0·40	,,	,,	
17	,,	,,	0·50	,,	,,	
18	,,	,,	0·60	,,	,,	
19	,,	,,	0·70	,,	,,	Not properly matured.
20	,,	,,	0·80	,,	,,	Not properly matured.
21	,,	,,	0·90	,,	,,	Semi-fused. Blibbed.
22	,,	,,	0·00	,,	2·67	Slight skin at edge.
23	,,	,,	0·10	,,	,,	
to			to			Good smooth transparent glaze.
27	,,	,,	0·50	,,	,,	
28	,,	,,	0·60	,,	,,	Pinholy transparent glaze.
29	,,	,,	0·70	,,	,,	Not properly matured.
30	,,	,,	0·80	,,	,,	
31	,,	,,	0·90	,,	,,	Semi-fused and blibbed.
32	,,	,,	1·00	,,	,,	

Type 2

ADDITIONS OF ALUMINA AND SILICA TO DIBASIC BORO-SILICATE

Table No. 3

	Molecular Composition					Results
No.	Na$_2$O	CaO	Al$_2$O$_3$	B$_2$O$_3$	SiO$_2$	E.F. Majolica Kiln
1	0·50	0·50	0·00	0·67	2·00	Part transparent, part opalescent.
2	,,	,,	0·10	,,	,,	Good glaze. Part opalescent.
3	,,	,,	0·20	,,	,,	Good glaze. Opalescent.
4	,,	,,	0·30	,,	,,	Good glaze. Faintly opalescent.
5	,,	,,	0·40	,,	,,	Good glaze. Smoother than No. 6.
6	,,	,,	0·50	,,	,,	Good glaze. Slightly pitted.
7	,,	,,	0·60	,,	,,	Glaze has tendency to dry edge.
8	,,	,,	0·70	,,	,,	Dry and blibbed at edge.
9	,,	,,	0·80 to 1·00	,,	,,	Blibbed and ruckled eggshell.
10	,,	,,	0·00	,,	2·33	Not properly fused.
11	,,	,,	0·10	,,	,,	Faint opalescent glaze.
12	,,	,,	0·20	,,	,,	Slightly opalescent glaze.
13	,,	,,	0·30	,,	,,	Opalescent glaze.
14	,,	,,	0·40	,,	,,	Good transparent glaze.
15	,,	,,	0·50	,,	,,	Good transparent glaze.
16	,,	,,	0·60	,,	,,	Good transparent glaze.
17	,,	,,	0·70	,,	,,	Semi-fused and blibbed.
18	,,	,,	0·80 to 1·00	,,	,,	Semi-fused, blibbed, ruckled.
19	,,	,,	0·00	,,	2·67	Semi-fused and blistered.
20	,,	,,	0·10	,,	,,	Not perfectly matured.
21	,,	,,	0·20	,,	,,	Opalescent glaze.
22	,,	,,	0·30	,,	,,	Opalescent glaze.
23	,,	,,	0·40 to 0·60	,,	,,	Transparent glaze, surface covered with minute pinholes.
24						
25	,,	,,		,,	,,	
26	,,	,,	0·70	,,	,,	Semi-fused, blibbed, skin.
27	,,	,,	0·80 to 1·00	,,	,,	Blibbed, skinned, ruckled.

Type 2

ADDITIONS OF ALUMINA AND SILICA TO DIBASIC BORO-SILICATE

Table No. 4

	Molecular Composition					Results
No.	Na$_2$O	CaO	Al$_2$O$_3$	B$_2$O$_3$	SiO$_2$	E.F. Majolica Kiln
1	0·33	0·67	0·00	0·67	2·00	Dry glaze of minute crystals.
2	,,	,,	0·10	,,	,,	Not properly fused.
3	,,	,,	0·20	,,	,,	Smooth dense opalescent glaze.
4	,,	,,	0·30	,,	,,	Opalescent glaze.
5	,,	,,	0·40	,,	,,	Transparent glaze.
6	,,	,,	0·50	,,	,,	Transparent glaze.
7	,,	,,	0·60	,,	,,	Not properly fused.
8	,,	,,	0·70 1·00	,,	,,	Semi-fused. Badly blibbed.
9	,,	,,	0·00	,,	2·33	Dull surface. Small bubbles.
10	,,	,,	0·10	,,	,,	Semi-glaze
11	,,	,,	0·20	,,	,,	Smooth dull glaze.
12	,,	,,	0·30	,,	,,	Semi-glaze.
13	,,	,,	0·40	,,	,,	Good transparent glaze.
14	,,	,,	0·50	,,	,,	Good transparent glaze.
15	,,	,,	0·60	,,	,,	Not properly fused.
16	,,	,,	0·70 to 1·00	,,	,,	Ruckled and semi-fused.
17	,,	,,	0·00	,,	2·67	Blistered dull glaze.
18	,,	,,	0·10	,,	,,	Semi-glaze. Tends to blister.
19	,,	,,	0·20	,,	,,	Smooth dull glaze, tends to blister.
20	,,	,,	0·30	,,	,,	Smooth dull glaze, tends to blister.
21	,,	,,	0·40	,,	,,	Almost matured.
22	,,	,,	0·50	,,	,,	Transparent glaze.
23	,,	,,	0·60 to	,,	,,	Semi-fused and ruckled.
24	,,	,,	1·00	,,	,,	

Type 2

ADDITIONS OF ALUMINA AND SILICA TO DIBASIC BORO-SILICATE

Table No. 5

No.	Na$_2$O	CaO	Al$_2$O$_3$	B$_2$O$_3$	SiO$_2$	Results E.F. Majolica Kiln
	Molecular Composition					*Results*
1	0·25	0·75	0·00	0·67	2·00	Dry and blistered.
2	,,	,,	0·10	,,	,,	Opaque and not perfectly matured.
3	,,	,,	0·20	,,	,,	Opaque glaze.
4	,,	,,	0·30	,,	,,	Opaque glaze.
5	,,	,,	0·40	,,	,,	Transparent glaze.
6	,,	,,	0·50	,,	,,	Transparent. Not perfectly matured.
7	,,	,,	0·60	,,	,,	Eggshell surface.
8	,,	,,	0·70	,,	,,	Eggshell surface.
9	,,	,,	0·80 to 1·00	,,	,,	Eggshell. Blistered skin at edge.
10	,,	,,	0·00	,,	2·33	Dry and blistered.
11	,,	,,	0·10	,,	,,	Not properly fused.
12	,,	,,	0·20	,,	,,	Not properly fused.
13	,,	,,	0·30	,,	,,	Opaque glaze.
14	,,	,,	0·40	,,	,,	Transparent glaze.
15	,,	,,	0·50	,,	,,	Dull surface.
16	,,	,,	0·60	,,	,,	Dull surface.
17	,,	,,	1·00	,,	,,	Dull surface.
18	,,	,,	0·00	,,	2·67	Dry and blistered.
19	,,	,,	0·10	,,	,,	Not properly fused.
20	,,	,,	0·20	,,	,,	Not properly fused.
21	,,	,,	0·30	,,	,,	Have smooth dull surface.
22	,,	,,	0·40	,,	,,	Transparent glaze.
23	,,	,,	0·50	,,	,,	Leather surface glaze.
24	,,	,,	0·60	,,	,,	
25	,,	,,	1·00	,,	,,	Dry and blistered.

GLAZE COMPOSITIONS
Tables 1 to 5.

$$\text{General Formula} \quad \dfrac{x \ R_2O}{y \ RO} \bigg\} \begin{array}{l} z \ Al_2O_3 \\ 0{\cdot}67 \ B_2O_3 \end{array} \bigg\} 2{\cdot}00 \ SiO_2$$

$$\overline{1{\cdot}00}$$

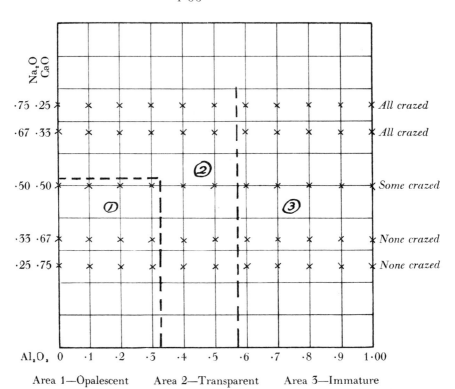

Area 1—Opalescent   Area 2—Transparent   Area 3—Immature

RESULTS OF THE EXPERIMENTS

Type 1. Previous to these experiments an earlier series had been made to determine the fusibilities of lead silicates. These ranged in ten successive stages from $PbO : SiO_2$ to $PbO : 2SiO_2$. The maximum content of silica that would fuse clear in the easy part of a

148

majolica kiln (see page 132) was about $1 \cdot 80$ SiO_2. $1 \cdot 90$ did not melt clear in the hard part of the kiln. $2 \cdot 00$ did not melt clear in the hard part of a glost oven. These present experiments and many confirmations of them later show that PbO, $0 \cdot 25$ Al_2O_3, $2 \cdot 00$ SiO_2 matures in the easy fire of a majolica kiln, and that PbO, $0 \cdot 25$ Al_2O_3, $2 \cdot 50$ SiO_2 melts clear in the hardest part of a glost oven. Hence the addition of alumina lowers the fusion temperature of lead silicates and thereby increases their capacity for silica.

Type 2. These experiments have clearly brought to light the function of alumina in this type of glaze.

1. It eliminates the tendency to opalescence.
2. It increases fusibility, i.e., lowers the temperature of fusion, and thus facilitates the maturing of glazes, and increases their capacity for silica.
3. It improves glaze quality. It is the medicine that maintains the general health of glazes by curing many defects.
4. Is neutral as regards crazing, but by virtue of (2), which increases the capacity of the glaze to absorb silica which in turn reduces crazing, alumina indirectly reduces crazing.

Alumina can be used up to a content of $0 \cdot 50$ and even $0 \cdot 60$ in cases where the $\dfrac{R_2O}{RO}$ content is not less than 1 : 1.

Type 3. The results of the experiments are in line with the results of the preceding two types. They too show that additions of alumina improve glaze quality, lower the fusing temperature, increase capacity for silica, and can be used up to a content of $0 \cdot 50$ and in many cases, $0 \cdot 60$.

Tables 1 to 5 have brought to light a very important factor in glaze composition. They show that the proportions of R_2O oxides and RO oxides (usually expressed as the relation of R_2O to RO) have an exceedingly important influence on glaze character. The chart on page 148 used in conjunction with the detailed information in the tables, brings out very clearly that variations in the relation cause great changes in quality, fusibility, transparency and opalescence, and *crazing*. In these matters alterations in the ratio have far greater effect than alterations in either alumina or silica content.

In the all important matter of crazing we see that:

Table 1 glazes were all crazed.

Table 2 glazes with $2 \cdot 00$ SiO_2 were all crazed;
with $2 \cdot 33$ SiO_2 some were crazed;
with $2 \cdot 67$ SiO_2 none were crazed when drawn from kiln. Some crazed later.

Table 3 glazes with $2 \cdot 00$ SiO_2 some were crazed;
with $2 \cdot 33$ SiO_2 none crazed immediately;
with $2 \cdot 67$ SiO_2 none were crazed.

Tables 4 and 5 glazes did not craze.

Thus demonstrating that increasing the ratio of RO to R_2O, (which is the same as reducing the ratio R_2O to RO), reduces crazing.

Incidentally, the experiments confirm that increasing the content of SiO_2 also reduces crazing.

The results of the investigation detailed in the foregoing pages are of inestimable value to the pottery industry. No comparable information was in existence before this research was undertaken nor does any such appear in later technical ceramic publications. It is not necessary to particularise other investigations in order to demonstrate the value of orderly methods of research. There is, however, one other matter worth mentioning. Methodical research is useful sometimes for correcting erroneous ideas. Thorough investigation of alkaline glazes is a case in point. Last century the prevailing idea was that the chief components of these glazes were but few in number, being mainly confined to an alkali (potash or soda); an alkaline earth (lime or baryta); silica, and the oxides of copper and manganese. Methodical research has shown that other materials can also be used with advantage—such materials as lead oxide, zinc oxide, alumina, borax, and even oxide of tin. Hence, the production of alkaline-glazed pottery similar to that made by Middle-Eastern potters centuries ago is not the difficult task it was formerly supposed to be.

EXPERIMENT AND DISCOVERY

The Lancastrian Potters were exceptionally prolific in discoveries. This was partly due to the times, for at that time the science of chemistry was emerging from a long twilight of imperfect knowledge and but few potters were making much use of it. The brothers Burton, being educated in the facts and principles of science, were amongst the earliest potters to apply them in their business.

Science contributed to the success of Royal Lancastrian Pottery in several ways. In particular she equipped us with a rich store of useful knowledge in the form of an orderly arranged inventory of nature's materials, and a systematic method of experimenting which enabled us to get a more intimate knowledge of the mysteries of the craft.

It naturally followed that the Burtons' pioneering with fuller knowledge and better methods caused them to forge ahead. Another factor was the stimulus of early and easy success. Joseph Burton's first recorded experiments were immediately successful by producing a glaze crowded with a myriad glittering crystals, and not long after this other experiments produced a very successful eggshell surfaced glaze. These successes came so easily that it seemed as if one had only to probe and something worthwhile would appear. Hence, experiments were continued with zeal and enthusiasm, and were rewarded from time to time with valuable discoveries.

A chronological record of important discoveries follows.

CHRONOLOGICAL RECORD OF
IMPORTANT DISCOVERIES

1893 Brownish coloured glaze crowded with a myriad glittering crystals similar to the Aventurine type of glaze discovered in 1884 at the Rookwood Pottery, U.S.A.

? A similar green coloured glaze.

1896 An eggshell surface matt glaze. The forerunner of the matt glazes now so extensively used.

1899 An antidote to prevent fritted glaze slip 'setting' to a sticky mass at the bottom of the container.

1901 The value of The Periodic Table to pottery chemists. No-one seems to have made systematic use of it before this date.

1903 An extraordinary glaze frit which gave on the addition of oxide of copper glazes with remarkable veinings, striae, and featherings. If oxide of iron was added in place of oxide of copper the glaze became crowded with beautiful reddish shining crystals.

1903 Zinc eggshell glaze by substituting an equivalent amount of zinc oxide for the whiting in the standard eggshell glaze.

1903 Magnesia eggshell glaze by substituting an equivalent amount of magnesia for the whiting in the standard eggshell glaze.

1903 Ultramarine Blue Glaze.

1904 Uranium Orange Glaze.

1905 Uranium Orange-Vermilion Glaze.

1909 Snow White eggshell Glaze.

1910 An eggshell glaze which gave a sky blue colour with a small amount of oxide of nickel and a green colour with a larger amount of nickel oxide.

1911 An intensely white brilliant glaze without using any opacifying agent such as oxide of tin.

1928 An entirely new way of decorating pottery whereby the artist's design is in the interior of the glaze and throughout its thickness. Known as Lapis Ware.

Pilkingtons' tile and pottery works, 1911.